SMART Man Hunting

SMART Man Hunting

How to Get Out There, Get Dates, and Get Mr. Right

Liz H. Kelly

Writers Club Press

New York   Lincoln   Shanghai

SMART Man Hunting
How to Get Out There, Get Dates, and Get Mr. Right

Writers Club Press
an imprint of iUniverse, Inc.

For information address:
iUniverse
2021 Pine Lake Road, Suite 100
Lincoln, NE 68512
www.iuniverse.com

Liz H. Kelly
Santa Monica, CA

While the examples given in this book are based on true stories, some of the details have been changed to protect the not-so innocent.

Edited by Marie Timell

Illustration by David Glynn

Author photography by Bader Howar

These strategies and codes are designed to bring levity and practical solutions to the modern dating scene for women seeking Mr. Right.

Visit www.smartmanhunting.com

ISBN: 0-595-24639-7

Printed in Canada

To My Parents

This book is dedicated to my parents, Anne and Phil, who met on a blind date and have been happily married for more than forty years. Your partnership inspired me to write this book and is a true model of love for anyone seeking a life mate. Thank you for giving me the courage to take chances, the confidence to build relationships, and the ability to have a sense of humor about it all.

Contents

Preface

When a divorce at thirty-five brought me back into the dating scene, I was amazed to discover how much everything had changed. Like most women, I wasn't sure how to meet men. And my divorce had left me doubting my own ability to evaluate whether someone could be the right partner for me. But I was sincere in my desire to give love another chance, I moved to a new, much larger, city and embarked on a Man Hunt determined to find the right partner versus someone to fill a void. I discovered that the dating scene had changed considerably since my twenties before I was married. I met many more divorced singles and Internet dating had become an acceptable way to meet men. It was a New Era. I needed to learn how to navigate it.

I realized that I had to completely change how I thought about the dating process. I needed to expand my thinking about how, when, and where to meet people. Luckily, the dating scene had changed a lot for the better when I was out of it. Because more people than ever are single, all kinds of new options for meeting people had opened up. The only thing keeping me from turning to these options were my own old-fashioned ideas about the "right" way to meet someone. Whatever those ideas were, they weren't working. My dating was limited and I knew it was time for a new strategy.

I began to realize that Man Hunting is a numbers game. You have to try to encounter as many men as possible before one will "hit." I knew I had to get out of my own zone—my area of comfort or what I call my Home Box. This meant I had to open myself up to all the New Era dating options: Internet Dating, Speed Dating, Professional Matchmakers, singles events and long distance dating.

I also had to prepare myself emotionally and mentally for my Man Hunt. First, I expanded my network of friends and turned to them for support and advice through my dating journey. Then, I gave myself a "Confidence Face Lift" and worked on my ability to take rejection. Most importantly, I adopted my "No Fear Attitude" to dating to achieve my goal of boosting my numbers, ego and odds of finding Mr. Right. Finally, one of my most important realizations came to me when, after working for three dot.com bombs, I found myself unemployed. Suddenly, I saw that finding a Man is a lot like a finding a Job and requires the same skill set.

My strategy worked! I was inundated with dates with all kinds of men. During my Man Hunt, I had four to seven dates a week and boosted my dating by 500%! Were they all good fits? No. In fact, I dated so many men—and in order to bring some levity to the whole process—I started to categorize them. My categories were a kind of shorthand for my girlfriends. Soon I'd call them up and announce that I'd gone out with yet another WD (Wounded Divorcé) or wonder why I wasn't meeting more BAs (Bachelor Available). Finally, as a party amusement, I formalized my categories in the form of twenty-six Codes and created an ABC Man Code Book. Word about the Codes spread. My girlfriends from all over the country began calling to know what Codes to assign their boyfriends and the men I know all wanted to know their type. All the positive feedback encouraged me to share them with a broader audience.

I also decided to view my period of unemployment as an opportunity to fulfill a long-held desire to write this book. Going back to High School where I was known as Dr. Liz, I've always coached my friends on their relationships. Combine this with a passion for writing and it seemed like the perfect time to throw positive energy into sharing everything I had learned about dating in the New Era with others. I especially want readers to expand their thinking and explore all the New Era dating options available because they really work.

In this book, I share with you my ABC Man Codes, a simple descriptive tool to identify the major types of men. This guide will help you size up what you've got on your hands and how to handle him. I have found that there are good guys, bad guys and maybe guys. By providing you with strategies, questions and true-story examples, you can make better choices and learn how to identify Mr. Right from Mr. Right Now.

My divorce was primarily due to the fact that I did not ask the right questions during the courting phase. Somehow I decided to overlook the clues regarding the potential for future conflict. I focused on our connections based on mutual interests in art and bike riding instead of differences in our value systems. After I was married for only six months, we found several disconnects as we dug deeper into what really mattered to each of us. While we parted as friends, we may have avoided the "D" word if we had taken a closer look pre-wedding bells.

I suspect the high divorce rate today is related to what went wrong for me. You have to fully evaluate whether someone is right for you not just on the basis of chemistry and similar interests but on whether he can be a LIFE Match. Dating is often twisted by hormones, age pressures, and the desire for companionship. A lot of heartache can be avoided during dating with a thorough interview process during the Dating Assessment Dance. As I dated, I learned how to say Next faster by identifying the red flags and observing their actions when meeting Man Candidates. Based on my thirteen years of interview training experience in the corporate world, I developed a way to obtain the most pertinent information about a Candidate's long term viability along every step of the dating journey. I also learned how to apply my marketing communications and sales presentation skills to achieve greater success in attracting the right men. In the end, though, you have to trust your own feelings. Finding Mr. Right is about combining you GUT instincts with the LIFE Match information you gather.

Whether you are looking for a good catch or advising single girlfriends, I hope *SMART Man Hunting* shows you how to prepare yourself to get out there, make the most of the New Era Dating Options available, and size up the man landscape in order to make the best choice for you. Remember, there are a lot of men out there and there's a Perfect Match for you. The Smart Man Hunting winning formula includes ways to stay balanced in your approach, maintain your confidence, know when to say Next, use the comic codes to keep your sense of humor, and keep dating until you find your Perfect Match.

Happy Man Hunting!

INTRODUCTION

What is SMART Man Hunting?

Are you tired of trying to figure out where the single, attractive, and available men hang out? Have you ever spent too much time focusing on Mr. Wrong? Are you ready to have some fun and be SMART about your Man Hunt?

New Era Dating

If you are a single woman seeking Mr. Right, you may have already realized that it's a whole New Era in dating. Thanks to the divorce rate, more people than ever, of all ages, are dating. While it may seem difficult these days to know where to find your mate, we're actually living in the best possible time for dating. Because of the sheer number of people looking, the 21st century has produced countless possibilities and new ways to meet a mate. And because of these new options a woman no longer needs to play the "gatherer" role, but can now proactively hunt for her man.

SMART Man Hunting is a dating guide that shows you how to use the New Era Options to seek out and meet Mr. Right, while saving you from spending weeks, months and years with Mr. Wrong. Why is the divorce rate at 50%? It may be that we women aren't making very smart choices about the men we pick (or allow to pick us!) or the way we go about it. For example, often women only look for boyfriends in very small ponds. By expanding our Home Box—our comfort zone—we automatically increase the number of available Man Candidates in our lives. The more candidates, the more likely you'll find the right one for you, rather than settle for the one who's there.

Second, nearly all women have been burned at some point. We all promise ourselves that we will be smarter the next time. But are we? How can we be without something to guide us? *SMART Man Hunting* provides you with a step-by-step approach to dating that shows you when to say Next versus when to take a closer look at the many candidates that the New Era Dating Options will provide you. Take the fear that you'll make another mistake out of dating and rest easy in the peace of knowing that *SMART Man Hunting* will show you the way.

SMART Man Hunting is based on interviews with hundreds of active daters (men and women), happily married couples, and my own experience gained from having hundreds of dates. It will help you find a man who thinks you are fantastic together with a long-lasting and meaningful relationship—everything most women desire.

What does SMART Man Hunting mean?

- SMART does not mean desperate.

- SMART does not mean aggressive.

- SMART means boosting your dating numbers, ego and odds of finding Mr. Right.

- SMART means, as a friend said to me, "Stepping out that door, taking chances, and testing new waters to find what you want."

- SMART means not putting all your eggs in one basket.

- SMART means demanding that guys treat you with respect.

- SMART means taking care of yourself and being surrounded by positive people who make you feel good.

- SMART means identifying red flags early and listening for clues so you can find Mr. Right faster.

- SMART means finding Mr. Right and avoiding Mr. Wrong.

The SMART Man Hunting Strategy

And as a wise 40-something girlfriend said to me, "This is the age of working smarter not harder. We all want to do everything efficiently. Man Hunting may not be politically correct, but we all know what it is."

So how are you going to get SMART about the hunt? Follow the guidance of this book. You'll find it is divided into four sections:

Section I "Get Ready for SMART Man Hunting"

This section helps you to transform your thinking and open yourself to New Era Dating Options. You no longer need to rely on your Home Box of friends, family and co-workers to bring you a man. Begin taking full advantage of New Era dating opportunities and acceptance shifts evolving in the new century. Chapter One shows you some new ways to think about yourself and the New Era, while Chapter Two prepares you to get "out there" by helping you to give yourself a "Confidence Face Lift" and to develop a "No-Fear Attitude." You're encouraged to approach your MAN Hunt like a JOB Hunt by using the same skill set. It also provides you with a Winning Hunter's Toolkit for your Man Hunt.

Section II "Explore the New Era of Man Hunting"

Many people are afraid to try Internet Dating, Speed Dating or Professional Matchmakers because as one wise man said, "It's like taking a fish out of water. People don't know what to do." This part of the book will tell you everything you need to know to survive out of the water. In-depth discussions show you exactly how to handle all the New Era Dating Options and how to make the most of them. What you should be looking for and dating safety tips are included.

<u>Section III "The Dating Assessment Dance"</u>

Once you start actively dating, Section III shows you how to assess, analyze and review the total man. Don't make the same mistake for the second or third time by not using all available means to closely evaluate potential partnership candidates. One 50-year-old man commented to me, "I am finding through my divorce that I married someone who I barely even knew." By using the Chemistry Connection Test, Candidate Interview Practices, and LIFE Match Questions together with an understanding of your own GUT and observations, you can make wiser Mr. Right choices and improve your chances of going the distance.

<u>Section IV "The SMART Man Hunting ABC Man Codes"</u>

This A-Z guide to New Era men saves you time and effort since it allows you to quickly size up and handle any candidate. Use these twenty-six comic codes to help you keep a sense of humor and quickly weed out the undesirables on your dating journey. The codes are based on true stories from women who have found great men, along with tales about being dumped, manipulated and taken for granted. We have all made mistakes. The goal is to know how to deal with any type of man, know when to say Next, and keep dating until you find someone who compliments your ABC codes as a Perfect Match.

In short, *SMART Man Hunting* is a New Era dating guide that helps you get SMARTer by showing you how to:

S   Search proactively for Mr. Right with confidence, using New Era dating options

M   Meet more high-quality men and boost your ego, while following SMART safety guidelines

A   Assess candidates to identify real deal LIFE potential in the Dating Assessment Dance

R   Review the Total Man, using the SMART ABC Man Codes and Final Man Analysis

T   Trust your GUT instincts and LIFE Match results to find your Perfect Match

Smart Man Hunting can also provide you with tips for life skills. You can gain new MAN and JOB hunting strategies. Using the notes gathered during my research, you can learn better ways to approach life from the people whom I met on the journey. You will not only benefit from new Man Hunting skills, you can live a "winner's life." And as a wise girl-friend told me, "Everyone wants to be with a winner."

Along with helping women on the hunt, men have found this guide to be a useful reminder for how to be SMART about hunting women. One male fan commented, "It's a book that puts all the best dating advice you ever heard but, sadly, forgot under one cover. I found the dating stories and, particularly, the codes to be a kind of useful shorthand for sizing up personality types–including my own."

Follow the SMART Man Hunting plan and you'll quickly boost your dating numbers, ego, and odds of finding Mr. Right.

SECTION I

*Get Ready for
SMART Man Hunting*

CHAPTER ONE

Transform Your Thinking

Are you ready to be proactive in your search for Mr. Right? Are you ready to try new man hunting strategies by thinking outside your Home Box? Are you ready to fill your life with happiness?

Throw Out Your Old Approach to Dating

In order to find Mr. Right, you will need to give some serious thought to how you've always approached dating in the past and start thinking about dating options outside your comfort zone or Home Box. Why? Because staying in your Home Box is why you are currently single. Finding the right mate is a numbers game. The more men you meet, the likelier it is that one will "hit."

Have you always thought that "fate" will bring you your mate? Do you go about your life thinking that "the one" will just cross your path? This strategy could be the reason why all your dates or relationships turn out to be Mr. Wrong. This dating strategy is called "Dating by Osmosis" and is equivalent to having no strategy at all.

One 34-year-old Marketing Consultant who met his mate at the car wash asked me, "What's wrong with meeting someone through osmosis?" Nothing's wrong with it. It can happen—it just doesn't happen very often. Your mate may be at the car wash, but Mr. Wrong and a few lunatics might be there too. Men are likelier to meet women through osmosis because it's a riskier strategy for women. We're less likely to be open to meeting people in this manner since it's in our interest to keep our guard up. For all you readers out there who have met dates "on the street" congratulations. For everyone else still seeking a high-quality mate, there are alternative winning search strategies for you here—so keep reading.

Get out of your Home Box

Your Home Box includes all your regular activities and relationships. It's your work, your friends, your family, where you live, and all your regular activities. It's where you live your life and feel most comfortable. It's also where you're not meeting any new men. Why? That's just the way it is. It could be that you've already dated the available men in your Home Box. Or you may have exhausted the supply of people your friends and family know to set you up with—that is, if you've even let yourself be open to this—more on that later. We all love to stay within the comfort and security of the home box. But if you're going to be a SMART Man Hunter, you have to move out from your home territory into new hunting grounds.

What's Stopping You?

You know as well as anyone that it's a New Era in dating. Everyone is dating. People of all ages are getting together to go out. Dating shows draw huge audiences on television. The media has broadcast all the new dating options available such as Internet dating and singles clubs. So why are you at home?

Overcome Your Old Fashioned Ideas About Dating

Here are some of the things that may be stopping you together with a few counter-arguments.

- *You think if you "put yourself out there" you'll seem desperate.*

Nothing is further from the truth. It's *not* actively dating that gives you that oh-so-slightly-desperate aura.

- *You've been out of the dating scene for a while and you don't know how to handle what might come up.*

Keep reading. This book is for you. It shows you exactly what to do on different types of dates.

- *Your judgment hasn't been so great in the past and you're a little afraid of your ability to make a sound choice in a man.*

Relax and let the experience of hundreds of active daters and happily married couples guide you. Arm yourself with Section IV's SMART Man Hunting ABC Man Codes and the Dating Assessment Dance steps in Section III and you'll rebuild your confidence in your ability to choose. And anyway, your choices in the past may have been influenced by the fact that you didn't have a choice. Get it? You took whatever came along. It's a New Era. This time around, you get to choose.

- *You're still recovering from your last relationship.*

Fair enough. You don't want to make the mistake of going out there before you're ready. Your heart won't be in it and you'll come off as needy or depressed or both. But, if you're reading this book it means you're heading in the right direction. Hang onto it. Take if off your bookshelf again when you *are* ready.

- *Your life or work is too demanding to allow the time and energy that a SMART Man Hunt requires.*

It's time to take a good hard look at your priorities. What's important to you? Career or love? You can have both but love requires effort too. Read on. You're an ideal candidate for the section, "Approach Your MAN Hunt Like a JOB Hunt." If career is truly your top priority right now—You Go Girl. But maybe this inclination is an excuse for something else. You may be in denial about whether you're ready for a relationship or not. Time to consult a counselor or at least spend some time thinking about yourself—provided you're willing to make the time to do that.

- *You don't think women should be proactive about dating. You consider yourself a "Rules" girl.*

But how can you be a "Rules" girl when there's no man to practice the rules on? You can still be a "Rules" girl and let the man take the lead if that's what you want. That still begs the question of how you're going to meet and assess men. Women who like the more passive role in relationships still need to open up the door for men to enter.

- *You're comfortable in your Home Box.*

That means you're comfortable being single too. You know the saying, "no pain, no gain?" Well it applies here. Sometimes you need to make yourself a little uncomfortable to move forward in life.

What Have You Got to Lose?

Besides what's stopping you, you might want to ask yourself what you think you have to lose by SMART Man Hunting. In other words, what are you afraid of? Assessing your fears and addressing them is very important if you're going to truly be proactive about dating. You have to adopt a No-Fear Attitude if you're going to put yourself out there.

Putting yourself out there is a necessary part of dating. Most men learned to put themselves out there at an early age since they have been traditionally trained to take the lead in dating. Aside from other reasons such as the differences in male and female psychology, this active dating strategy could be why all your exes always seem to "bounce back" and find someone again so quickly after your breakup. They just seem to know what to do to meet women. Well it's time women learned what to do to meet men as well.

Adopt a No-Fear Attitude

Do not be afraid to get out in the New Era dating playing field. Adopt a "No-Fear Attitude" and be prepared to deal with rejection. Yes, rejection is part of the game. But rejection is a fact of life. Give yourself a pep talk about it. How many times have you been rejected and survived only to discover that the rejection was the best possible thing for you?

Remind yourself that you have no control over what makes someone attractive to someone else. Usually it's a combination of chemistry and psychology. Just because you don't have that chemical/psychological hook that makes someone want you doesn't mean there's something wrong with you. In any case, different people are looking for different things in relationship.

This time around be SMART and keep the focus on what you want and are looking for in someone. And stop worrying about what someone else wants. I've met men who never called me back after our first meeting despite the fact that I felt a connection. I learned very quickly not to take the rejection too seriously and to just keep saying Next! If the guy was not wild about me, then why torture myself trying to make it work? I was tired of torture.

With *SMART Man Hunting,* you'll learn to let rejection roll off your back and to not take things too personally. This No-Fear Attitude is actually an important skill in love and work. Overly-sensitive people who fear rejection are a pain to have to tiptoe around. If you can eliminate this unflattering quality from your repertoire, your bosses and boyfriends will be grateful for it. An upside to SMART Man Hunting is that it gives you an opportunity to practice. In SMART Man Hunting, you'll be able to deal with rejection because the rewards will be much greater than the losses.

Play the Numbers Game

Remember that the whole idea behind SMART Man Hunting is to broaden your choices in men by working a numbers game. Men have done it for years so why shouldn't women use this approach? The more men you date, the better will be your options and ability to make a sound choice for yourself. But this numbers game has another upside. Not only will you be meeting more men, but you may be making friends and business contacts along the way. Not everyone will be a "keeper," but some of the people you meet may work for you on other levels. As a result, your Home Box keeps getting bigger and bigger. At this point, osmosis may even work for you.

When Does Osmosis Work?

Osmosis works when you are dating actively and not desperate. Osmosis works when your Home Box has grown to include new people and activities. Relying solely on osmosis gives you that needy attitude that makes men avoid you. Stepping outside of your home dating box of friends, family and work makes you more open-minded and boosts your ego. When you are being proactive about dating, you might just find him when you least expect it. Osmosis yes, but not as your one and only strategy.

Transform Your Thinking Wrap Up

Hopefully, by now you're convinced and ready to begin SMART Man Hunting. You're willing to leave your Home Box and adopt a No-Fear Attitude. You're prepared to learn how to bounce back from rejection and to not take things personally. Using this "out of your comfort zone approach to dating," I have found more high-quality men and made great business contacts along the way. By mining for gold and bouncing back from rejection, I have felt much happier and enriched as a person.

An important part of SMART Man Hunting is to adopt a positive attitude and be confident. Chapter Two shows you how. When you're confident, you'll be amazed at the good things that come your way. By using this SMART Man Hunting technique, you will be beaming with confidence and become a magnet for men simply by the way you approach life. On your Man Hunt journey, you might discover that Mr. Right is someone you already know. He may just enter into your life through osmosis. Alternatively, this guide is about getting out there, taking chances, boosting your ego by actively dating, and being SMART about your selection process. In the end, you might find natural synergies bring you and your life partner together. But by then, you'll have a wealth of dating experience and man analysis to draw upon. You can do it! Remember, No Fear!

Chapter Two

Boost Your Confidence

So you've decided to take the plunge and start to Man Hunt the SMART way. Hopefully, Chapter One convinced you to get out there and be proactive about dating by taking advantage of all the New Era dating options available . Chapter Two is about making sure that your dating journey starts off on the right foot in order for success to be assured. If you are not finding high-quality mates, recognize that it may be time to make some changes. Take a timeout, give yourself a Confidence Face Lift, and then go find your man!

So, before you go out there cold, let's do some preparation. Like the beginning of any endeavor, it's always a good idea to do some self-assessment and review.

The first step is to take a look inside and be open to making adjustments. Be honest, and ask yourself some tough questions:

Personal Assessment Questions

- Am I really happy with my life?

- Do I have a good support network of friends and associates?

- What are my personal interests and hobbies?

- Do I set aside enough non-work or play time for myself?

- Am I taking care of myself—mentally and physically?

- What's my approach to life? Am I generally positive or do I project a negative attitude?

- Do I feel secure about the way I look?

- How do people tend to respond to me? Are they genuinely happy to see me or hear from me?

- Do I make sure that I'm given respect by everyone in my life, including my dates?

Even one "no" to any of the above questions could mean it's time to make a few changes in your life. And if you're not sure about the answers to these personal assessment questions, start asking your close friends for some honest advice. While one of the biggest things you can to do is decide to open yourself up to all the New Era Dating Options and to begin Man Hunting the SMART way, you may also need to make a few other changes in yourself.

Give Yourself a Confidence Face Lift

A 30-something girlfriend commented to me, "It's all in your approach. Project a positive attitude in your dating journey and you will find success." Have your dating experiences been more in the nature of disasters than dreams? Building or rebuilding your confidence can solve a lot of your current dating troubles. A wise 37-year-old girlfriend once told me, "Confidence is the greatest sex appeal." If you are truly happy with your life, the world will line up to meet you.

Confidence is everything in the dating game. Here's why. Confidence:

- Is Sexy!

- Lets men know you like yourself and won't put up with nonsense

- Means you know there are many men who are anxious to go out with you—which only makes you more attractive

- Is when you take rejection lightly and not personally

- Allows you to relax and enjoy the dating process

- Makes it clear that you are not desperate—the date killer

- Makes dating fun

- Means you're happy with yourself, your looks, and your life

So how do you paint a smile on your face? Why is it so important? Another friend gave me excellent advice. She said, "Guys have basic requirements. They want someone who is happy and confident." If your confidence has taken some pummeling lately, try my Recruiter girl-friend's advice. She told me, "Fake it until you make it because nobody wants to be near someone who is not confident." You want everyone to say, "I want to have what she's got." People will naturally want to meet you if you are glowing with positive energy.

Try These Confidence Boosters

When I started gathering these confidence building tips from friends—both male and female—I was inundated with good ideas. That just goes to show you how important it is to present self-assurance and a positive attitude. If you try some of these tips, you should have more confidence and be more comfortable with yourself. Here are some confidence boosters and reminders:

- Recognize that you are a hot ticket item with unique qualities who deserves only the best. If you need to be reminded of your positive attributes, ask your friends to help you. While you may not have everything on someone else's checklist, you do have great key selling points that make you special.

- If you're not happy with your looks, do something about it. Get a new haircut or makeover, join a gym and get back into shape, or get serious about losing a few pounds. Do whatever it takes to maintain your body's best image. One 40-year-old girlfriend told me, "Love your body just the way it is today." You don't need to have plastic surgery to find a man, but you need to maintain an appealing presentation.

  If you are not sure what needs to be done, ask your close friends. What might be a painful conversation at first can bring you ultimate success in the dating arena. By making a commitment to be at the top of your game physically, you'll feel more confident and men will come your way. For example, my closest confidant and neighbor told me, "Your hair is too bleached blonde. We have to tone it down." She sent me to her hair stylist one hour away and, wow, it was worth the drive! In addition to fixing my color, the stylist also recommended new makeup and lipstick.

- Eliminate the friends or associates who don't give you the appreciation you deserve. Who needs people around who are tearing you down when you are trying to build yourself up?

- Try something new. Go out on a limb and try something you've always wanted to do. Take a Tai Kwon Do class, go horseback riding, or take a ski lesson. Don't do these things to meet a man—yet. Do it for you to show yourself you can learn some new tricks.

- Pamper yourself. Have a facial, get a massage or manicure, take in an art exhibit. The idea here is to do something nice for yourself, something that makes you feel good.

- Treat yourself better. Make sure you take your vitamins, drink enough water and eat right. Get out in the fresh air once in a while. These things are basic but you'd never believe how many people ignore this stuff.

- Finally, the best confidence booster is to have a dating plan and to stick with it. The more you date, the better you'll feel. Handling all the different situations that arise in your dating journey will also reinforce all your new positive feelings about yourself. Remember, no fear.

Make Dating Positive

Now that you've given yourself a Confidence Face Lift, it's time to talk about your SMART Man Hunting dating approach. It's always best to know what your approach is going to be and to arm yourself with what you expect or hope to achieve before you try on some of the New Era dating options or even go out with someone you met by osmosis. The key is to be positive.

1. Be Comfortable With You

This comfort level isn't just about your renewed confidence, it's about not trying to twist yourself into shapes because you think that's what your date wants. One 30-something girlfriend told me, "Relax and be yourself around potential soul mates." She added, "Don't dress up to fill the part that you think he wants you to be." By being yourself, your smile will be more natural and pronounced. By wearing what makes you feel good or doing what you enjoy, you will be more attractive. Don't try to fit anyone's mold because you will always lose in the end.

2. *Know That You Can Take It or Leave It*

While you want to show interest if you feel any, don't think you have to move forward with someone just because they are interested in you. At the earlier stages of dating, there isn't a whole lot invested emotionally. If someone isn't what you're looking for, don't continue on. Cut your losses early. Remember that you can leave it. Don't have a scarcity consciousness and fear that no one else will want to go out with you. There's always more from where that came from.

3. *Follow a No Bull Policy*

Set boundaries, respect yourself, and do not put up with any more bull. You deserve the best and do not tolerate anything less. One 50-something woman commented to me, "Think about the people who make you feel really good about yourself. Surround yourself with people that give you the same feeling and respect. You will be much happier." If the guy is constantly late picking you up, talking on the cell phone during dinner, and making excuses, you know where to run. Remember, "Next…"

4. *Take Advantage of the New Era Dating Ratios*

Believe it or not women have the numbers advantage in the New Era dating scene. This advantage has evolved with demographic shifts and the fact that more men are willing to try these modern options and wait until later years to find a mate. One 30-year-old male friend told me, "I decided to stop Internet dating because the odds are in the favor of women." He added, "I think the ratio is ten to six males to females on some Internet sites, which makes it tough for men to win."

5. *Don't Let Go in the Bedroom Too Fast*

Another 40-year-old male entrepreneur said to me at the coffee shop one day, "Women have the power to control the world because they are the ones that determine when to have sex. You need to tell all your girl-friends to go slowly with sex and they will always win." Remember, you want him to think you are the hottest ticket in town. Let him get to know you and show his appreciation before you let go in the bedroom.

A 45-year-old actress told me, "I told my fiancé that I needed to sleep on the couch the first night that I slept at his house because after only three dates it was too early for me to stay in the same room. He completely understood and it made it more special when we did decide to be with each other." By taking a slow approach to intimacy, she actually made their bond stronger and now is planning her wedding to this 50-some-thing executive.

6. Approach Man Hunting as an Opportunity to Have Some Fun

Above all, try to have some fun on your journey to find Mr. Right. Do not take every initial meeting so seriously. Learn to laugh at yourself, and share funny moments with potential mates. If you are nervous or anxious during a date, no one will want to come back for more. Remember, if something does not work out, there is another opportunity waiting for you around the corner. One girlfriend pointed out to me, "Men are like buses. A new one comes along every ten minutes."

Boost Your Confidence Wrap Up

With your renewed confidence and new approach to dating, continually remind yourself that you are a unique and special person who deserves a top-gun partner. Don't be nervous on your Man Hunt. Wear a big smile, be patient and relax because the right one will eventually come to you.

You will find that the Man Hunt process is similar to a job search. Hopefully, you have a few job hunting skills that can help you navigate the New Era dating playing field. Compare your MAN Hunt to a JOB Hunt in the next chapter.

Chapter Three

Approach Your MAN Hunt Like a JOB Hunt

MAN hunts are very similar to JOB hunts. You may not like this idea since it doesn't satisfy your more romantic notions of love, but the sooner you accept this notion as a simple fact, the sooner you'll be dating. If your feminist instincts don't like the idea that you're looking to fill the job of wife, don't think of it that way. Look at it as though you're simply making sure that the broadest number of opportunities (dates) are placed in your life for evaluation. You want to be sure to find a job which is the best fit for you right? It's the same with dating.

When I found myself unemployed, I decided to conduct parallel searches for a MAN and new JOB. The unemployment rate was at the highest level since 1994 and I had left a Vice President position. I prepared mentally for the "over-qualified" stamp, assessed my savings, and started creating my search strategies. Instead of waiting for the JOB and then finding a MAN, I decided that life is too short and it was time to seek both. One 40-year-old dot.com founder told me, "Your approach is perfect for finding a MAN and a JOB."

When looking for a MAN or a JOB, you're using the same set of skills and strategies. Keep these in mind as you search and you'll end up a winner.

The Winning Hunter's Strategic Plan

In order to win in your Man Hunt as well as your life journey, here is some advice from happy and confident people who steered me down a success path. These winning strategies form a coherent plan of action and can help you find a MAN and/or JOB:

1. Define your Requirements

Whether you are seeking a MAN or JOB, you need to at least start out with a few parameters concerning what you are seeking. It helps to define your ideal situation. A woman I know, who met her husband on the Internet, gave me this advice: "Target Market." Her point was that by defining what you want, you can find him faster. (More on this can be found in Chapter Nine "What You Should Know Before You Go.") By being clear about what you want, you'll avoid wasting time with Mr. Wrong. Later, I remind you to stay open, but if you're looking for someone with the same education level as you and that's a Masters degree, there's no point spending too much time with a fitness trainer with a degree from massage school. Even though your Man Hunt may take you down surprising paths in the form of guys different from your original vision, it is helpful to know what you truly want in a MAN upfront. In other words, what are the deal breakers for you?

Try to be realistic about your requirements. An older and wiser 50-something girlfriend—who is about to get married—emailed me the following: "I look at a relationship in a very different light than I did ten or fifteen years ago. I don't need someone to complete me, save me, or be me. Getting to that place gave me a whole new world of possible candidates."

2. Be Patient and Persistent, Not Desperate

I met with a 30-something male Executive Coach who told me that my best job hunt strategy was "patience, persistence, and don't take things too personally." There are many parallels to my man hunt strategy that apply to this job search advice. Just getting out there once or twice is not enough, you have to keep trying. Eventually something is going to click. Be prepared for rejection (see previous section,) and persistently knock on doors. Do not give up until you meet your goals. Another friend pointed out to me, "It is important not to be desperate when looking for a job or a man."

3. Check Your Needs at the Door

I approached each first date interview or job networking event in a very light-hearted fashion to avoid giving off needy vibes. Neediness implies desperation. If the shoe were on the other foot, would that be attractive to you? Try to figure out what's making you feel needy or desperate. Then remind yourself that you have plenty of time and that lots of opportunities are waiting for you. (Review the "Confidence Boosters" in Chapter Two.)

One morning I walked into a major healthcare firm for a breakfast networking meeting. The host kicked off the session by sharing, "We decided to hold these smaller meetings because the organization's members found the larger events exhausting since they got bombarded with requests for jobs and consulting work." When we went around the table to share names and interests, I decided to try a new strategy. I stated with a smile, "I am here to learn from you and promise not to harass you for a job. I am unemployed, but really came to learn new buzz words to help me prepare for future interviews."

You know what happened after the meeting? I received three potential job leads. Not acting desperate and letting people get to know me without pressure achieved a much better result for me than otherwise. By lightening up and using a sense of humor, I had much greater success. The same holds true for dating. If you respond to your Mr. Right candidates with a light approach, they will want you more. One 50-something woman said to me, "Just play nonchalant. Just say, O.K., fine, no problem when they say they are busy." With this non-desperado style, your man is much more likely to come running after you.

When I date, instead of giving off needy and negative vibes, I keep myself busy with positive activities and friendships that make me feel good about myself. The perfect positive project for me was writing this dating book. I also continued taking my piano lessons with a "no pressure to be Beethoven" approach, participated in a book club, and frequently got outside for walks on the beach and hikes in the mountains. I learned to laugh at my mistakes, and just keep getting up in the morning and plunging forward with the MAN and JOB hunts.

4. Don't Try to Force Things

Pressure to close a deal too fast is related to being needy. When we are over-anxious, we might take too much of a lead in the dating process. In other words, don't be pushy. Let things unfold naturally and you'll be much happier with the result. One wise 50-year-old male non-profit CEO told me, "We're not twenty anymore. If it's a real deal, you don't need to direct your romance because it will build naturally."

Another 40-year-old male friend said to me, "It's important to let the guy lead." By taking a non-needy and patient approach, you can easily let the guy lead. Let him make the first calls to action and then respond favorably if you are interested. Even with Internet dating, you can let the guy take the lead. (And only if you are interested, no feeling obligated just because someone likes you!) If he is not interested, just keeping saying, "Next." Remember, the trick is to be SMART, not desperate.

While it may feel frustrating to give up control over how a date or relationship is progressing, you'll win in the long run. Every time you want to exert control, try turning instead to something that is truly within your control. Do your dishes, pay your bills, work out, or visit a friend. Your dates would thank you for it.

5. Bounce Back from Rejection

Yes, I got rejected every day on both the JOB and MAN hunt fronts. I had to learn how to bounce back quickly when countless recruiters told me, "You're over-qualified." Even though I reached out to my network of friends and contacts, many times they did not call me back right away. I decided that my best approach was to maintain a positive attitude, use my sense of humor to add levity when I did talk to people in my network, and just keep trying. People are busy, and my job hunt was not everyone's top priority.

Paralleling these job hunt rejections, I met many Mr. Wrong candidates on my MAN hunt. I set up coffee with men who seemed to be Mr. Right candidates only to discover that they had lied about their age or that the photograph of themselves they'd posted on the internet had been misleading. I was also stood up once because I was not SMART enough to catch some red flags. As I started making changes in my expectations and assumptions by learning from these mistakes rather than being disheartened by them, men lined up to meet me and the job offers started coming my way. Remember mistakes are valuable lessons and will only make you SMARTer.

6. Let People Know You're Looking—Ask for Help

Although I received many rejections, I also got lucky many times—usually when I asked for help. As you broaden your horizons, you'll be meeting many new people. Just like in a Job Hunt, you shouldn't be afraid to ask people to help you. Often you don't even need to ask, people will offer it to you. But this won't happen if you don't tell people you are looking for a MAN or a JOB. It pays to be open.

For example, I set up a lunch meeting with an Internet industry contact to brainstorm job search ideas. We shared job hunt strategies, but I also mentioned that I was writing this book. Then she told me, "By the way, I am a published author and can talk to you about how to get your book published." If I hadn't stepped out and asked this woman to lunch, or opened up and talked about my book, I might not have ended up with a great book coach.

I also sent out a group email to my friends announcing my MAN hunt. You would be surprised how many people replied with Mr. Right candidates. The opportunities are out there, but you might need to ask to find them.

7. Use a Give-and-Take Approach

JOB and MAN hunts are also give-and-take situations. There is a lot of truth to the statement, "What goes around, comes around." You need to offer your contacts and ideas to people. When you share what you know, you will be surprised how much more willing people are to help you in return.

While seeking a JOB or MAN, I also look for opportunities for my friends and business contacts along the journey. If I hear about a job lead that might not be for me, but can help someone else, I try to connect the parties. When I was working I took unemployed people out to lunch almost weekly to help them brainstorm job ideas. Guess whom I called when I lost my job? Similarly, if I meet a MAN that I like, but don't feel a love connection, I often offer to set him up with a girlfriend who may be a better match or invite him to a singles event.

8. *Keep an Open Mind*

Be open-minded in your travels and while networking because you never know who will introduce you to whom. You are bound to have something in common with most of the people you meet and there is some value in almost every connection. For example, my 30-something girlfriend met a 65-year-old man on a plane. He later introduced her to his best friend's son. At the very least, all the characters you encounter will further help you define what you want. Everyone can show you a new side to yourself and teach you something new.

9. *Avoid the Perfectionism Ferris Wheel*

During the course of your Man Hunt journey, it is important to remember that people are not perfect. If you are searching for a one hundred percent match, you will quickly fall into a "Perfectionist Paradox" and never make a decision. This state ensures an endless ride on a Ferris wheel with no results. A 50-something Marketing executive who is happy in his second marriage told me, "Marriage is about finding the person you love so much that you can live *with* their faults."

No matter what ABC Man Code (see Section IV) or other category your date might fit into, you must learn to accept people for who they are and determine whether or not their character meets your needs. The LIFE Match Game described in Chapter Twelve will help you make a final decision.

10. *Evaluate the Candidates*

Finding a life partner should be taken at least as seriously as seeking a new job. Early in the dating process, prepare your interview questions in advance to determine if it's worthwhile to proceed to the next step with someone. If the candidate makes it to the third date, you can start using the LIFE Match Questions found in Chapter Twelve to further evaluate his core. In order to narrow the field, use Section III "The Dating Assessment Dance" as your guide. Pay attention to red flags and heed their warnings. If you see major hurdles that would have to be overcome, be willing to move on to the next candidate. A 35-year-old male colleague told me, "One of the biggest mistakes that I see women make is they fixate on fixing a guy versus moving on." Make, "People Don't Change," your mantra.

11. *Make Friends and Don't Burn Bridges*

At this point, I have dated many men and can attest to the fact that the majority of those relationships settled into friendships and nothing more. This outcome is not surprising given that we are all looking for a specific combination of elements in a potential life partner. The challenge to find the right match is all the more reason to get out there and increase the number of men you meet. You might date any number of men more than once, getting to know them in a deeper way, but not proceed to the next level. It's always best to strive to maintain an ongoing friendship even if a romance doesn't work out.

I met two men through Internet dating who both ended up being great business connections. One candidate offered to share my resume with his top-gun friends at a major telecommunications company. The second potential candidate asked me to partner with him on a consulting deal for a wireless company. While I did not want to continue dating either of these men, I initially contacted them because we had similar interests. As a result, I ended up with two job leads.

Remember, it is a small world. Keeping your associations positive is even more important in the New Era. You might find that a candidate-turned-friend will one day help you find a job—or a mate. One 30-something girlfriend commented to me, "I always try to end things on good terms. We originally came together for a reason and that connection is what's important." You never know when your paths will cross again so try to part on a good note.

12. *Pace Yourself*

Similar to a job hunt, you shouldn't rush around frantically in your search for a Man. While you will be surprised by all of your dating activity once you approach dating the SMART Man Hunting way and use the New Era dating options, remember to pace yourself. You don't want to show up on your dates exhausted. You want to be at the top of your game for every interview. I made the mistake of trying every type of option at once. This climaxed during one week when I went on seven dates. Afterwards, I retreated to my support network of friends and told them, "I cannot keep going out with strangers. I need to see you for dinner and take a timeout." Once I pulled back from my Man Hunt efforts and resumed a better balance, my smile returned to my face.

Approach Your MAN Hunt Like a JOB Hunt Wrap Up

This chapter demonstrated that you *can* achieve success and meet Mr. Right by choosing to date proactively and approach your MAN hunt like a JOB hunt. You need to leave your Home Box and be ready, willing, and able to meet new people by opening yourself to New Era dating options. You've learned how to bounce back from rejection, maintain your smile, exchange ideas and not give up. I shared this thought about the journey with my friends: "I feel like I am playing the lottery. You just have to keep playing and eventually something will hit."

Get Ready for SMART Man Hunting—You're Armed and Ready

So how do you put all this information together in one hunter's winning package? Here is a simple tool kit for the next phase of your journey—getting out there. And don't just get out there. As one 39-year-old male musician told me, "You have to play to win."

The Winning Hunter's Tool Kit

- Change your ideas about dating and be willing to leave your Home Box.

- Prepare for the hunt by building your confidence.

- Define your Mr. Right requirements and keep them realistic.

- Be patient, not desperate, and keep your sense of humor.

- Bounce back from rejection and don't give up.

- Ask for help and use a give-and-take approach.

- Keep an open-mind and get off the Perfectionism Ferris Wheel.

- Pace yourself and don't burn bridges

You are now a Confident, Sexy and SMART Man Hunter, so it's time to get out there and explore the Man Hunting Landscape.

SECTION II

Explore the New Era of Man Hunting

CHAPTER FOUR

The Man Hunting Landscape— Expanding Your Home Box

With your new Man Hunting approach, winning strategies, and confidence beaming across your face, you can now start benefiting from the substantial number of New Era dating options currently available. With the preparation of the previous section in place, you are ready to venture out and find a soul mate.

Don't be afraid to try new dating avenues. Your Man Hunt journey can only be enabled by modern technology and demand-driven dating providers. There are millions of wonderful people out there using the New Era dating options, and you might just find your man using new search engines. While I definitely hesitated trying Internet dating, Speed Dating and Professional Matchmakers at first, once I jumped in the game, I met many intelligent and interesting people out there.

You can also find Lawyers, TV Producers, Management Consultants, Commercial Real Estate Brokers, Marketing Managers, National Account Managers, Writers, Teachers, and Doctors. The majority of these candidates had the same objective—to find a special someone. So I encourage you to try one or several of these options if you are still seeking Mr. Right. Simply by getting out there and boosting your dating numbers, you will significantly increase your odds of finding your man.

What New Era Dating Options Are Available?

New Era Dating Options are the direct result of both the rapid development in communications technology and evolving attitudes regarding the "right" way to meet a mate. Most of the benefits of the New Era wouldn't be in place if it weren't for the creation and global expansion of the worldwide web. Meanwhile, high divorce rates and failure rates in relationships have created tremendous demand for new ways to meet people. Technology and human ingenuity stepped in to fill the gap—to everyone's benefit.

The main advantage of New Era dating options is that they allow you to broaden your dating spectrum. Remember, finding Mr. Right is a numbers game. You can find thousands of Mr. Right candidates via Internet dating sites, quickly meet available men through Speed Dating, and conduct more thorough searches using Professional Matchmakers. In addition to enabling the proliferation of New Era dating options, technology has transformed the world of dating in other ways as well by making the world a smaller place. It's easier and more pain-free than ever to not just *search* for but to *connect* with someone. Today, it's quite effortless for friends to set you up via email introductions to likely candidates. It's possible to become reacquainted with old boyfriends with whom there's still a spark. Through email correspondence and flirtation, you can maintain long distance romances or meet a diverse group of international business travelers. I met a 70-year-old woman who told me, "I've re-connected with an 85-year-old man. We email each other coast-to-coast on a regular basis and I am so in love that I may need to move back east." She was beaming from ear-to-ear.

Survey the Land—Expand Your Home Box Beyond Friends, Family and Work

A wise 56-year-old male executive told me, "Life is about updates. You need to constantly update your approach to work, friends, family and dating." If you look beyond traditional dating approaches, you will find endless dating opportunities.

Remember that the first order of business is to get out of your Home Box. Even if you may not be ready to start using the New Era Dating options, it's good to get out and survey the territory. You might want to start your Man Hunt by easing into it. Comfortably expand the boundaries of your home turf by changing your regular routines and associating with some new people. Try something new or learn something different—anything that shakes up your world a bit. You could take a yoga class or sign up for a photography class at a local college. This kind of "sticking your toe in the water action" will also engender confidence. Even if you are ready to plunge ahead and turn to the next two chapters that describe all the New Era dating options in further detail and how to best use them, it's never a bad idea to simultaneously work on Home Box expansion, so read on.

Jump into your Passions

Think about your favorite hobbies and get more engaged in some of those passions. Sign up for activities and associations that you enjoy so that you can easily meet people who share the same enthusiasm for your interests. If you like golf, go to the driving range to expand your network of friends. Join a ski club if you like exploring the slopes. Not only will you meet new people, but you'll build the confidence that powers your sex appeal by doing the things that make you happy. As a result, you might just meet Mr. Right on your travels.

My 37-year-old piano teacher actually met her husband at tango dance lessons. She had not dated anyone seriously for three years, loved to dance, and told me, "I was horrifically lonely, so I decided to take classes as a way to meet people." After their second class together, she had a date with her 49-year-old entrepreneur dance partner. The couple went salsa dancing on their first date and never looked back. They were engaged ten days later, moved in together at three months, and then she became pregnant at seven months. During her first contractions, she decided that it was time to formally tie the knot before the baby arrived. The couple ran to the Court House for a fast wedding and then to the hospital for delivery the same day. Simply by stepping out and jumping into her passions, she was fortunate to find "the one."

If you notice that your favorite activities tend to be populated by mainly women, try an entirely different approach. While a book club might give you joy, you probably won't meet Mr. Right there either. A very wise 30-something woman, who was recently married, gave me some great advice regarding activities for meeting men. She started with this observation:

- "A lot of women do stupid things recommended by women's magazines to meet men—things like taking a pottery class or trying to run into divorced dads' grocery carts at the supermarket. This is ridiculous. The men to women ratios for fun outdoor sporting activities are really far more favorable for single women."

She continued with these tips for activities where the odds are in the female favor:

- "When I was doing a lot of climbing, I signed up for a weekend ice-climbing course. There were two women and about thirty men. I got a lot of attention. Of course, it is not a good idea to sign up for something like this just to meet men. You should like the idea of learning about ice climbing. Kayaking is another good sport. Typically, ratios on rivers hover around seven men to one woman. If you are more of an indoors person, rock gyms are also good. Most of the guys you meet at these places are great. They are outdoorsy, adventurous, well traveled, fit and they want to talk to you because they are sick of being around other guys all the time. A word of warning: these types of guys definitely do not fall for the 'helpless me' routine so don't be too prissy."

Build your Foundation of Friends and Community

Another move outside your Home Box is to consistently work on expanding and diversifying your foundation of friends. Diversifying your associates exposes you to many new outlets and people. But, never neglect your core group of intimates and supporters, they are the ones who will see you through the Man Hunting process and will build your backbone.

In addition to this foundation, be ready to expand more socially into your community to meet new people. You never know who might connect you to "the one." While I have a great core group of friends, I have also made countless contacts at the neighborhood coffee shop and through hobbies and business contacts. By being open-minded to people's suggestions, you might be surprised what this approach can do.

Simply by listening to a 40-something lawyer's advice in the coffee shop, I ended up testing Speed Dating for this book and as part of my Man Hunt. Not only did I meet a Mr. Right candidate at this event, I got a lucky break by being interviewed by Los Angeles' KNBC 4 News about my experience.

Another way to become more involved in your community is to engage in community activism or service work. You'll be doing something good for someone else or promoting a cause in which you believe. It stands to reason you might meet someone with similar interests and concerns as you. I volunteered for my neighborhood community association, and as a result, ended up swapping notes with a fellow board member who hosts a cable talk show on relationships.

Friends and community are success keys for your Man Hunt journey.

Technology Expands Your Home Box

You can immediately start benefiting from the use of email, cell phones, calling cards, personal organizers, pagers, the Internet and text messaging technology. These advancements have created new courtship technologies that can help you expand your search.

Email enables you to increase your bandwidth through far-reaching and free correspondence. Flirt with your man candidates using new technologies. For example, one of my top men candidates sent me a text message on my cell phone right after my first piano recital. The message was cute and simple: "Hi Liz, How was the recital?" How many points do you think he gained with this move? I sent him a warm reply.

Lastly, frequent flyer miles and modern communications have made international partners and long-distance relationships more feasible in the new millennium. Don't discount a long-distance man. If it is meant to be, you can make it happen—with a lot of help from email.

Use Email as a Dating Enabler

What did daters do before email? Essentially, email enables all New Era dating. You no longer need to wait for a party and hope to meet someone face-to-face there. Nor do you need to hope that there's enough time at a party for you to get to know someone who introduces themselves to you. Today, friends can set you up via email with contacts all over the globe.

Because my parents were set up on a blind date by college friends, and are still together more than forty years later, I welcome email introductions by friends.

While the old-fashioned blind date rarely included communication between the couple before the fact, email enhances the New Era dating process by providing a means to share information before you even lay eyes on one another. You can now compare interests, values, and even photos prior to a live encounter. I was set up on a blind date through a mutual friend via email that was a big success. My friend emailed both of us positive notes about each other and recommended that we meet. Since we both shared similar interests in the relationship business (he works for an internet dating site), it was easy to strike up a dialogue with this guy. After our first date, I discovered that this male candidate spends a few weeks a month in Munich, Germany, for business. However, I was willing to give it a shot because there was clearly chemistry, similar value systems, and a mutual desire to explore a committed relationship. This communication medium allows you to easily broaden your search without geographic limitations.

As part of your SMART Man Hunting Strategy, a phone conversation can complement email communication before your first date. Sometimes it can be difficult to determine the tone if you rely solely on email. While email is a timesaver and works great with busy people, it cannot completely replace live contact.

A word of caution about email blind dates: You don't want to wait too long for an in-person meeting either. For example, my 40-year-old girlfriend was introduced via email to a 37-year-old candidate through a mutual friend. Even though she lives in Los Angeles and he resides in Baltimore, Maryland, the two exchanged emails several times a day for about three months before their first in-person meeting. While my girlfriend felt that she knew this candidate fairly well after months of email exchanges and a few phone calls, there was no Chemistry Connection when they finally met. In the end, she commented, "It was a total waste of time because I waited too long to meet him and then there was no physical attraction." The two parties were not even interested in maintaining a friendship.

Email introductions by friends can open many doors and increase your search bandwidth. However, it is important to have live contact sooner rather than later and keep your expectations in perspective so you avoid time wasters.

EMAIL FLIRTING

Once you have established a connection via email introductions, international mixing, Internet dating, Professional Matchmakers, Speed Dating, singles events, or long distance connections, email can be a great way to keep the flame alive. Email flirting is the new substitute for written correspondence. The old-fashioned letter courtship has returned with the advent of the Internet. The majority of individuals now have at least one email address that can be used for personal communications.

You can use email effectively to flirt with your Man Candidates without interrupting their busy schedules. Email is non-intrusive because he can respond when his clock allows. The receiver can decide his emotional response to the email and respond when ready.

In today's modern world where extra personal minutes are at a premium, a brief email is far more efficient than a phone call at work. Nearly everyone has a PC at work or at home these days, which makes it easy to send short notes via email during the day.

Even an extremely hard-working candidate no longer has a valid excuse for a lack of communication. Anyone who is not regularly communicating should be taken off your Man Candidate list immediately.

The new technology has made it so easy to communicate using email and cell phones that there is no reason for a lack of regular contact anymore.

Men also like email flirting because it takes the pressure off cold-calling women for dates. I met a man from Italy who recently moved to the United States. This 33-year-old film editor told me, "Email is the greatest way to test a woman's interest." Several of his test messages turned into exciting dates, he said, and one resulted in a long-term relationship.

While there are many benefits to email flirting, watch out for misinterpretations and substituting other forms of communications too soon. The tone of an email is often hard to judge, especially if sarcasm comes into play. Different personalities can present more challenging results from email flirting. Many men also tend to send short Joe Friday-type ("just the facts") emails, which can be easily misunderstood. Consequently, I recommend email flirting as only one part of the courtship equation. Regular phone contact and face-to-face communication cannot be totally replaced by email when building a connection.

Expanding Your Home Box Wrap Up

As you open yourself up to New Era Dating Options, remember that the success key is to continually expand your Home Box. Engage in new interests, focus on diversifying your foundation of friends, and open yourself to your community.

Above all else, start to use the vast array of technology out there to broaden your bandwidth. Today, you practically can't date if you don't have email. So, if you still don't have a computer, find a friend who will let you use his or hers. Or investigate the local library or Internet cafés in your area with Internet access. You'll have to establish a private Internet address with an email provider that can be accessed from anywhere. That's pretty easy. Even if you have internet access at work, it's always a good idea to set up a private account so you can keep your personal life personal. Now that you're engaged proactively in your Man Hunt and you're armed with the necessary tools in the form of confidence, a dating toolkit and email, are you ready to enter the New Era of dating? Are you ready to enter the web?

CHAPTER FIVE

Enter the Widest Web

Have you ever sat home and wondered, where all the good men? Wonder no more. Because everyone works longer hours with limited amounts of free time today, candidates and seekers are adopting new dating entry vehicles. New Era daters are accepting these new ways to meet candidates because they greatly expand their search for Ms. or Mr. Right. Have you ever considered trying Internet matchmaking to find a man? This option is now a socially-accepted way to meet your mate. By taking advantage of the New Era dating trends and tools and meeting dates on the Internet, you can create a SMARTer approach to the Man Hunt.

Stepping into Internet Dating

I was initially hesitant about taking the plunge and using Internet matchmaking sites to date, but a close 40-something male friend encouraged me by saying, "It is like walking into a room with thousands of strangers and instantly finding people with whom you share common interests and goals." I was nervous at first, but decided to go for it. I discovered that women definitely have the demographic advantage here. Even though many people are not willing to publicly admit they have tried it, more fish are jumping in this wide ocean than you'd think. And because there are so many more men online, you really cannot pass up this opportunity as a woman.

A happily married couple who met on the Internet shared their encouraging story with me. She is a 40-year-old Accountant who married a 42-year-old Financial Manager in Washington D.C. While she was in the process of moving to Washington D.C. from Arizona, she met her soul mate online. When I asked about what initially drew her to him, she said, "I liked the conversational tone of his emails. He wrote about Al King and it made me laugh." Both of them had been Internet dating for months without finding a mate.

The couple discovered many similarities and hit it off immediately. For example, they both had grown up in Phoenix and attended Arizona State. After three emails and two phone calls, they decided to set up a date. After the first date for drinks in Arlington, Virginia, they became almost inseparable outside of the office and agreed to date exclusively. She explained their relationship progression to me: "We shared our likes and dislikes and life experiences with each other." Within five months, they were engaged, and married at the end of eleven months. The Accountant's advice to you: "It's a numbers game. The more you put yourself in situations where you can meet people, the better your odds of finding the one."

Another woman I know, a 33-year-old single mother also met someone special through Internet dating. Not only did they share similar professions and an interest in sports, he was intelligent, adventurous, considerate and very attractive. On their first dinner date she commented, "I knew that he was high-quality when he offered to pay for the babysitter." The couple dated for approximately two years, and now maintains a friendship.

A girlfriend commented to me, "I think the Internet is the number one way for the 45-to 60-year-olds to find someone today." She expanded by telling me about two couples who met over the Internet in their 50s and 60s. She explained, "The first couple is a 56-year-old nurse who married a 56-year-old broker. The second couple is a 60-year-old widow who is in a long-term relationship with a 64-year-old retired doctor."

No matter what your age, the Internet provides dating results. But you have to be patient to find Mr. Right. You may not meet him right off the bat, so don't be discouraged. Eventually, you will find some very viable high-quality candidates. Take the experience of this 35-year-old woman who told me, "I went out on forty-eight Internet dates before I found my man, but now we have been happily married for three years."

The Ego Boost Benefit

While, initially, you may not want to step into the Internet dating scene, there are many rewards to trying this approach provided you use the Net SMART Safety Tips (more on this later in this chapter.) One 38-year-old Business Development Manager finally convinced me to take the plunge by saying, "It's flattering to receive so many emails from men. The experience is a big ego boost."

How can you benefit from the Internet Ego Boost? Well, first of all, the Internet will show you that there are plenty of men out there interested in meeting you. This attention is especially helpful if you've been suffering from a loss of hope or feelings of frustration over how to meet men. By successfully meeting and dating a variety of men, many of whom will be interested in you, you'll experience the "Internet Dating Ego Boost." Online dating increased one girlfriend's confidence so much that she attracted a soul mate that she met at a car wash! By setting low initial expectations, she avoided being disappointed and found the ego strokes to be invaluable. When she signed up with an Internet dating service and posted a personal ad online she received approximately fifteen emails per day in the first week, which eventually slowed to three emails per day at the six-week mark. She never had to initiate contact because her inbox was flooded with solicitations from inquiring male minds.

One of my girlfriends, who is actively Internet dating, told me, "I taped a sticky note on my phone that says 'The Ego Boost Benefit' after reading your book to encourage me to keep dating." Are you ready for an ego boost?

The Internet Dating Process

So how does Internet dating work? The best way to Internet date is to sign up with an Internet matchmaking service. These web sites allow you to scan personal ads posted by men or to post your own ad for a fee. You can either write to someone whose ad you like or you can wait to see who writes to you. The benefit of the site is that it keeps all correspondence between you confidential. Neither one of you has to know anything about the other that you don't want to reveal. So, if you correspond with someone and choose not to continue the correspondence, he'll never know how to reach you again. There are many sites out there, you just need to find the one for you. Simply run an Internet search for "Internet Dating Services," and quite a few will come up. There are all kinds of sites, matchmaking sites specific to certain religions (Christian, Jewish, etc.) or even specific to certain interests such as skiing or writing. Each one has unique characteristics, so investigate a bit and even ask your friends which ones they like.

SITES AND STRATEGIES—MY EXPERIENCE

After two years of resisting Internet dating, I finally decided to step into the arena and eventually tried five different Internet dating sites. Each site had a different personality and approach. I share my experiences with each service, but I'm not you, so I recommend that you try several yourself to discover which one provides the best results for you.

- ***Slow Start:*** I decided to start out safe and slow. The first site, *The Right Stuff*, was aimed at Ivy League graduates. I felt more comfortable using this venue as a starting point because the service's screening process was more extensive. You needed to mail written proof of your graduation from an Ivy League school prior to being placed on the site. Unfortunately, I only received a few responses and went on two dates in six months. The mechanics of the site were not made for easy online matchmaking and I needed to find more action. So long, Ivy League.

- ***Join the Crowds:*** I decided to venture into a more broad-based site, *Match.com*, and was overwhelmed by the response. I received more than two hundred emails in the first month alone. I also learned quickly about the female demographic advantage in the Internet dating arena. In comparison, a male friend of mine who is a 34-year-old actor told me, "I haven't received any inquiries from women in two months."

- ***Test Drives:*** After interviewing a 52-year-old friend for this book about his online dating experience, I decided to try a one-week trial subscription with another more popular site, *Matchmaker.com*. I received forty responses during the first week on this third site. Based on my previous experience, I was also more prepared to handle the selection process for all the emails I received. What distinguishes this site is that it has additional communications options beyond emailing candidates, such as sending someone a "wink" by using the icons on your account.

In addition, I tried a two-week free trial on a fourth Internet dating site, *Blinddatetv.com*. This site allowed me to block emails from bad guys. I felt safer with this feature and used it when I came across IPs (Internet Psychos). You can read more about these crazy men in Section IV's SMART Man Hunting ABC Man Codes.

- ***Personality Test Route:*** After interviewing an active female dater for this book, I also checked out a site called *eHarmony.com* that sets up singles based on a series of personality test questions. It took me a few hours to set up the profile, but it was a great exercise. While chemistry is the unknown and the lack of it is a showstopper if there is no connection, the personality plays just as important a role when making a match so I was willing to give it a try. After you complete the tests, the service sends you a few good matches and advises you to "treat them like gold." If you like the brief description of the guy, you can start engaging in several stages of correspondence that includes additional multiple-choice and short-essay questions regarding your likes and dislikes. If you make it to the final stages, you can then start sharing photographs, free-form emails and phone calls. While I had to drop out of the game due to the fact that I had too many Mr. Right candidates at the time, my girlfriend met with three men and felt a connection with all three whom she met using this personality test route. Because of her 100% success rate, you might want to take the time to try this site out.

The Net Steps Process

After you've found a site you like, follow these steps:

1. Enter by Registering for an Internet Dating Service

You can easily sign up as a member or just test out an Internet dating site. Most Internet sites have a similar protocol. You will be given a username and password to protect access to your information. You will be asked to enter a credit card for payment or sign up for a free trial. Most dating sites have free trial periods so you can take a test drive for one to two weeks and determine whether this vehicle works for you before paying anything.

2. Write an Enticing Personal Profile

While you will be asked to complete a series of multiple-choice questions about your vital statistics (age, age range that you want to date, interests) for your personal profile, use the essays as a marketing tool to entice suitors. The essays usually include a brief description of you and what you are seeking in a mate. Make your descriptions light-hearted, short, and include at least one interesting attribute to attract men and ignite email introductions. Remember, you want to maximize your selection by boosting your numbers so make every word count in a personal profile! Before you post your profile, you might want to run it past a girlfriend or, even better, a male friend for an objective view as to how it comes across. Ask them to be honest, does your profile make you attractive and bring out the best in you?

3. Add at Least Two Recent Photos

Ask a girlfriend to take some current photos of you. Either use a digital camera or have the photo scanned onto a disk so you can upload it onto your computer. Upload a photo that makes you look good, but it should also be realistic and look like you. It's horrible to meet someone for the first time who looks nothing like their online photo. You will have more success dating online with a photo and it's even better to add several pictures with different viewpoints. Photos of you engaged in your hobbies can also help build bridges. Outdoor hobby photos that include sailing, hiking and biking will especially attract more men to your profile. Don't worry about adding a photo because no one will know your name unless you decide to tell them.

4. Receive a Flood of Emails from Men

Once you set up the profile, you will probably find yourself singing, "It's raining men." There are so many more men than women trying Internet dating that the odds are in your favor. If you do not receive a big response initially, go back to your girlfriends or close male confidants and ask for more feedback on your profile. Sites actively promote new members so you should be overwhelmed in the first month. Eventually, the flood will recede and the stream of emails becomes more manageable. Updating your profile periodically will also stir up more activity if you find yourself in a lull.

5. Screen the Emails and Man Resumes

Similar to hiring an employee, your next step is to screen the emails you receive. When email introductions spark your interest, consider the man resumes by reviewing their profiles to search for top-notch candidates. Determine your man selection criteria and then scan their profiles to determine who should be eliminated from contention immediately. (See a more in-depth discussion on "Weeding Through Email" later in this chapter.) You are now ready to write back to anyone who makes the cut.

6. *Make Email Contact with a Few Good Men*

Once you find a few good men, send them short and sincere email responses. Try making a comment about something in their profile. For example, you might write, "I saw that you like to travel. What is your favorite place to visit?" You will find that a short series of emails follows if there is sincere interest on the part of the candidate. I also recommend keeping emails short with some humor (you don't want to go overboard with the sense of humor or you might be misunderstood) to preserve your energy in this initial stage. You may share something too personal in an email right out of the gates only to never hear from the other party again. If his responses are sporadic, eliminate him. This passive approach is a sign of lack of interest.

7. *Move Towards Phone Contact or Move On*

At a certain point in your email correspondence with a candidate, he may ask for your phone number. If there seems to be a connection and you'd like to speak to him on the phone, respond with a request for his number instead of giving out any personal information of your own. If you are interested and the candidate doesn't seem to be moving to the next phone step, eliminate him.

8. *Pick Up the Phone for a Pre-Screening Call*

Don't be afraid to call the guy. He wants you to call if he gave you his number. However, be SMART and safe when you place the call. Use Caller ID blocking (*67) to protect your privacy so your phone number won't be revealed on his Caller ID on the first call. Then go for it. But remember, SMART women are not aggressive or desperate so keep the call casual and light. You are simply pre-screening the candidates similar to pre-screening employees. Don't spend hours on the phone telling him your whole life story. You might waste a lot of energy only to be disappointed when he doesn't ask you out for coffee. If you do set up a time to meet, he might show up looking like a completely different person compared to his profile, which is another reason to limit the first phone calls to a minimum. Simply listen to his tone of voice and test whether the conversation is easy or a struggle before deciding whether you want to accept an invitation for a first date from a guy.

9. *Setting up Coffee Talk*

After you have weeded out undesirable candidates via email and the phone, you may be ready for face-to-face contact with someone. If you click on the phone with the Man Candidate, the next step is to set up Coffee Talk. (See more in Chapter Ten.) You can let him make the call to action (where he suggests that you meet in person) and then agree only to meet in a safe neutral place. I recommend a coffee shop because it is safe and alcohol-free. (Alcohol will blur your ability to assess the candidate. Employers don't interview job seekers while drinking, do they?) Don't pick the shop on your block either. You are not ready to give out your address at this stage. Suggest a public meeting place close-by, but not where you will bump into the neighbors or could be followed home.

10. *Take the Chemistry Connection Test*

When you meet for the first time, relax. You don't have to prove anything to anyone. However, it's in your best interest to be dressed for success since he could be Mr. Right. Be courteous and interested in what he has to say, but this is *your* evaluation. If you are not drawn to his personality and physically attracted to him, the deal is over. He will be doing the same thing, so don't feel guilty. The bottom line is that your primary concern should be to ask yourself, "Do I want to kiss this guy?" You can read more about First Date Tests in Chapter Ten.

11. *Accept a Second Date if He Passes Go*

If he passes Go and you realize that you might want to kiss him, let him schedule a second date. Wait for his call. Don't call him. Men like to take the lead in the early stages of their Woman Hunt so let him make the suggestions and figure out the details for the second date. If he does not call, it is okay. Move on to your next candidate and don't take it too personally. Remember, you do not want to be with someone unless he thinks you are the hottest thing out there.

12. *Third Encounters and Beyond*

Once you agree to meet him for a third encounter, expect a more proper date. Meet for a walk in the park, drinks, dinner, or any other plan he suggests. Just keep it safe by not having him pick you up at your house and not letting him take you home. Continue to keep your home and work addresses confidential. If subsequent dates aren't well-planned in the sense that he calls you last minute, suggests something tacky, or is too quick to get you into his house or into yours, eliminate him. Remember, many guys use a third date rule as a goal to get you into the bedroom. You want to at least pass this milestone before you let your guard down.

If he continues to pass Go on subsequent dates, start asking more questions, take your time getting to know him, observe his actions, and get the facts. See more on this topic in Quick Qualifiers and Showstoppers in Chapter Eleven. Also, start to look at him closer by using the LIFE Match questions in Chapter Twelve and the SMART ABC Man Codes in Section IV.

13. *Identify Mr. Right Candidates*

If he makes it past the third date, then you are dealing with a Mr. Right candidate. You do not necessarily need to drop all other offers or grant more access to yourself or your life, but it is time to start asking tougher questions to uncover any true partnership potential using the LIFE Match Game. You are about to engage in the Dating Assessment Dance and should consider this discovery period an exciting part of the Man Hunt journey. Refer to Section III for more resources to help you to identify Mr. Right.

Weeding Through Email—The Net Selection Process

Once I was up and running in the Internet dating world, friends wondered how I sorted through all those emails to separate the wheat from the chaff. It wasn't that difficult. Based on my experiences and interviews with female friends, here are some tips on narrowing the Internet dating field.

Here's what I found effective when sorting through Internet dating emails from male candidates:

- *Eliminate Impersonal Men* My first step was to eliminate anyone who seemed obviously insincere. Usually these men only looked at the photo and clearly had never read my profile. That included the many men who sent me poems and sales pitches without my name in the introduction. These guys are engaging in mass email campaigns and their cast-a-wide-net-and-see-what-gets-hauled-in strategy is beneath consideration. These electronic form letters deserve to go the way of all junk mail. One girlfriend commented to me: "If all they write me is, 'Hi Sally, you are cute, check out my profile and let me know what you think,' then I delete their inquiry."

  An email introduction from a man should indicate that some thought went into its composition. It should demonstrate that the author actually read your profile and considered it by expressing interest in a mutual hobby or belief. If a candidate makes a sincere effort, then you can proceed to check out his photo for a chemistry test.

- *Look for a Chemistry Connection* The next step is to check out someone's photo. The best photo profiles include multiple pictures with headshots, hobby shots and full body views. A word of caution should be added here because I discovered that many men lie about their age and use misleading old photos. You might want to ask them about the age of the photo if you are suspicious. Look for hobby or vacation shots and ask them to tell you more about when they participated in the hobby or visited the remote location depicted to suss out the age of the photo. Style of hair and dress are also giveaways for dated shots.

If your Internet suitor is wearing a hat in his photo, chances are that there's nothing growing under it. While baldness was not a deal breaker for me, others might feel differently. In addition to the hat trick, several men may provide pictures of themselves with dark hair. However, when you meet, you may find them to be completely gray.

If someone only posts a head shot photo, he may be hiding something about his body. Double check the height and weight listed in his profile to see if the numbers add up. If someone states that he is 5'10" and weighs 250 pounds, you may want to ask for more photos before meeting in person.

Don't overlook the importance of the photo as the first step in testing the Chemistry Connection. One 37-year-old Marketing executive told me, "I first focused on reading the profile and then looked at the pictures later." While she found men with similar interests, they often failed the chemistry test. As a result of these failures, she shifted her selection process to checking out the photos first.

While everyone tries to put his best image forward in Internet dating profiles, nothing can completely replace the in-person meeting for a more reliable Chemistry Connection Test.

- *Beyond the Checklist* Once you have established some mental and physical connections based on his email and photo, the next step is to further evaluate whether your interests, priorities, and personality match via email. I created a few key questions that I would ask several men and then compare their responses. For example, I often asked about their favorite country, because international travel is important to me.

  I also asked Man Candidates to describe their ideal day to see how they might want to spend it with me. If the candidate liked getting up at 6:30 A.M., I knew this man was out because I am not a morning person. If the candidate responded that his ideal day consisted of having sex five times with me, I realized he was pretty much looking for one thing and that this was a bit forward for my taste. However, I connected well with the active types who enjoyed hikes, museums, movies, and cuddling by the fireplace in the evening.

- *End Communications with Perpetual Emailers* Beware of the Internet dating candidate who is a perpetual emailer. These men will email back and forth with you until your eyes cross, but somehow never find the opportunity to call or meet for coffee. Set a limit for this first phase of Internet courtship. If it seems that your candidate would rather be a pen pal than a suitor, move on. This behavior could be a sign that a man is only in it for the entertainment value, Married But Available (MBA) (read more about these men in Section IV), or otherwise emotionally unavailable.

  One 39-year-old executive girlfriend told me, "I was often frustrated by men who never wanted to make the first move to ask for a phone number or suggest coffee." She exchanged emails with one candidate at least five times and there was no effort on his part to connect on the phone or meet for coffee. While he wrote eloquently and they seemed to share many similar interests, she just had to stop writing when it was clear their interaction wasn't going anywhere. He never followed-up, and it left her with an empty feeling when the correspondence ended.

- *Beware of These Other Red Flags* In addition to the Net Selection Tips above, there can be any number of red flags in those first early emails. It pays to look for them. Here are a few warning signals:

  - Spelling errors and poor grammar. This guy lacks education or is too lazy to be sure his writing is correct. Next.

  - Brings up sex. That's what this guy is looking for. Next.

  - Writes a long heartfelt letter. This guy is needy. Next.

  - Too much information. You do not need to know his whole life story when you haven't even met in person to test the chemistry. Next.

  - Talks about his ex. Avoid men who share details about their ex in your initial email exchange. If he is bringing it up, he is probably not over her. Next.

  - Asks you about your ex. Men don't need to know about your ex in the early email stages. Everyone has a past and you are obviously over it or you would not be Man Hunting. Next.

  - Recites the resume. Is he trying too hard to prove himself to you by listing his life achievements in emails before a first date? You don't even know if you want to kiss him. Next.

Watch out for these email red flags and you can save hours of your time and energy focusing on the wrong guy. If you see these warning signs, don't be afraid to just say "Next."

THE MALE PERSPECTIVE ON INTERNET DATING

During my research, I received hundreds of comments from men about the Internet dating selection process. Here are two representative samples of male thinking on the topic.

Bachelor #1's Internet Dating Story

This 36-year-old Consultant found his wife through Internet dating. After using advanced search features, this man found five most likely to succeed candidates and ended up with a life partner.

The couple found an immediate connection. After two weeks of dating, he knew she was "the one." He described his mate as, "34-years-old, never been married, and an excellent communicator." He likes the give-and-take dialogue in their relationship and says their discussions are "balanced versus competitive."

Bachelor # 1's Internet Dating Advice

- Avoid long and demanding descriptions of what you are seeking in a partner.

- Avoid too much detail about yourself in your profile because it can be overwhelming.

- Provide a general description about yourself with enough information to spark an interest.

- When writing, keep emails short when corresponding with potential Man Candidates.

- Be open-minded and approach your search as an adventure.

- Do not use a sexy picture unless you are only seeking sex.

Bachelor # 2's Internet Dating Story

I also interviewed a 47-year-old Fundraiser who has been dating using the Internet for some time. While he hasn't found a long-term commitment yet, he has found several relationships by Internet dating.

Bachelor # 2's Internet Dating Advice

- Use more than one photo of yourself. It's easy to find one good shot, but multiple photos can present a better all-around image. More photos put men at ease because they sense that they know what they are getting.

- Don't feel intimidated or embarrassed of your age. There are plenty of men looking for peer-aged partners.

- Try to match education levels. Because this candidate is well-educated and worldly, he seeks an intellectual partner who can share his interests.

- Be truthful about your statistics. You want to hook up with someone in person eventually and the truth about your height, weight, or age will come out. What's worse, being rejected by a stranger because of who you honestly are or being rejected after someone's expressed interest in you because you turned out to be dishonest?

- Try to put some thought into the essay in your web profile. The idea is to give someone a sense of who you are without getting too personal. Bachelor # 2 told me, "I reviewed the essay answers for signs of someone who was curious about the world, had a sense of humor, and was naturally centered." While these qualities are not always easy to detect, he said, "You can eliminate the obvious opposites."

Net SMART Safety Tips

Now that you have some insight into the Internet Dating selection process, you should also review these SMART safety guidelines. While the worldwide web can open you to all kinds of new men, it can also expose you to men whose intentions may not be honorable or, worse, who are mentally unbalanced. Remember not everyone has the same value system as you. Be cautious when dealing with strangers and take pains to shield your privacy at all costs.

While Internet Dating requires the most security, these safety guidelines can also apply if you met the man through chat rooms, singles events, Speed Dating or Professional Matchmakers. You need to proceed with caution and protect yourself when dealing with strangers. While you enjoy all the benefits that the New Era dating options offer, let these safety tips guide you through email, phone and live contacts.

1. Be Anonymous When Emailing

First of all, any matchmaking web site will give you an account that allows you to stay anonymous. So don't use anything that could identify you when you share your email address. Second, I recommend that you set up an email account that also uses an anonymous name. For example, if you have an email account you use to talk to friends, family and business associates with your name in it, such as "lizhkelly," then do not use this account. I created a separate email account to handle my Man Hunting correspondence under a totally different name that couldn't be used to identify me. Just figure out any kind of fictitious name or "handle." If you'd like, you can use an address that reveals something about yourself such as a hobby or personal attribute. For example, my email address was tied to my interest in sailing. One of my male candidates used "greeneyes" as his email address, which helped him stand out in the crowd.

2. *Be Anonymous When Checking Email*

If you are dealing with an experienced computer whiz, you may also run into privacy trouble when using the Internet. One 34-year-old programmer showed me how he adds a link to his personal website with a tracking ID within his Internet dating solicitation emails. He was not receiving many Internet dating responses from women and wanted to see whether anyone was checking out his website.

Using this tracking ID, he obtains all kinds of information if you click on the link to his website and check out his photographs. He can actually look up the registered name and address for the IP address that you use to access his website. If women click this link from work, he told me, "I can actually see the name and address of their server." He has the information coded so that he can tell who, when, where and how often someone checks out his website photos.

How can you protect your privacy from this type of tracking guru? By clicking on a link to a personal website from a dial-up or cable line that is not connected to a business or school, chances are that he will only find the address for a central server and you are safe. However, if you make a habit of clicking on links with tracking IDs from the office, you might encounter an Internet Psycho (IP) and end up with a surprise visitor at work. While this security breach example is extreme, my programmer friend told me, "Only one woman was ever smart enough to look up the registered address for my website." It's time for us to get SMARTer when using 21st century technology!

3. *SMART Phone Contact*

After several safe email exchanges, you can cautiously move to the next Internet courtship level. Arrange time to speak with your suitor on the phone and see if he passes the verbal test. Because you are still dealing with a virtual stranger, you should use safety guidelines for connecting on the phone. First, ask for the guy's phone number and use Caller ID blocking (*67) when you call him so that your phone number is not revealed to him. You can even use Caller ID blocking on most cell phones so always try using*67 when placing first calls.

If you are ever at the point where you are comfortable giving out your phone number, use a cell phone or alternate number to your home phone. If someone is really creepy and has your home or work phone number, he can track you down using reverse telephone number lookups. Avoid such a situation by taking extra precautions when giving out personal phone numbers.

Trust your gut instincts when you talk to someone on the phone. If someone makes you feel the least bit uneasy or puts you off in any way, eliminate him. It won't get better if you meet in person. Remember there are plenty of other candidates out there. Next.

4. Continue to Put "Safety First" When Making Live Contact

Once a verbal connection is established on the phone, you can schedule a live meeting. I recommend that you always have these meetings in a public place and make sure you are familiar with the area before you agree to the location. Meet the candidate at the designated venue— never rely on someone you don't know for a ride. Don't even accept a ride home even when you feel as though a candidate is on the up and up. If you drove to the meeting, avoid allowing the candidate to walk you to your car. It's best to even keep the make, model, and license plate of your car a secret. My favorite meeting place is a local coffee shop, but not one too close to home. If you schedule a lunch or dinner date, use valet parking when possible so that the candidate, who is primarily a stranger at this stage, cannot follow you to your car when you leave.

Lastly, hold your cards close to your chest. Be careful about the amount of information you share during these first meetings and phone calls. Never give out your last name or address until you are comfortable with someone's character. There are women who have been stalked and even raped by Internet dates, so you just can't be too careful in the beginning.

5. *Consider Man Background Checks*

If you are curious, there are many ways to find out more about man candidates. Internet search vehicles can help you find out details about candidates prior to meetings. By searching on the man's name, you can easily gather information about his background. For example, if you use *Google.com*, you might find out about his educational degrees, work history, and personal interests. You can also click on the "Groups" button to learn more about his interests and hobbies. Other options are also out there. You can check genealogy sites for his family history. And if you get serious with a man, you can even go to the extreme of hiring a professional investigator to check out his history more thoroughly.

CAUTIONARY TALES—STORIES FROM THE FIELD

No matter how hard you try to be smart and safe, you will probably run into a few wild cards along your Man Hunt journey. While you can meet these men through any dating avenue, there seems to be a higher likelihood on the Internet. You might think you know someone after a few dates and then he turns into a totally different person. Many women shared stories with me about rude, emotionally unstable, and sexually aggressive men who use the Internet simply to get laid. Beware of these jerks, watch for the warning signs, and get out fast.

- I interviewed a 43-year-old Production Coordinator who had been Internet dating on and off for three years. While she has had two long-term relationships from Internet dating, she also had to weed out a few wackos. She told me about two first dates on which the guys "forgot their wallets." Wallet MIA # 1 was a successful 45-year-old land developer who announced he'd forgotten his wallet upon arrival. She graciously offered to pay for the date even though there was no Chemistry Connection. She added, "I do not need to be taken out to dinner. I'm happy to meet for a walk on the beach or a cup of tea, but this guy had insisted on meeting at the restaurant." They never saw each other again.

  The second time she was not as nice. She met Wallet MIA # 2, who was a 48-year-old real-estate professional, outside his home for their first date. They walked a few blocks to an expensive Italian restaurant that he had selected. At the end of dinner, he announced that he had forgotten his wallet. In this case, she did not offer to pay. The guy finally spoke to the hostess, who told him to walk home and get his wallet. He was embarrassed and angry, and she never saw him again—nor did she care. She commented to me, "I hate cheap men because I am not cheap. They don't have to spend a lot of money, but should be kind and honest."

- Another 37-year-old Marketing Manager told me about a 42-year-old pornography-industry jerk whom she met on the Internet. He had disguised his career, claiming to be a writer, but confessed to her on the date that he made porno films and was seeking "A conservative woman who wears an apron." This wacko proceeded to quiz her with a list of ethical questions. For example, she said that he asked, "What household chores do you like?" and "If I asked you to have sex right now in the bathroom of this bar, would you do it?" He left after an hour to go to a "porno-related business meeting," and she was relieved to see him leave.

- The most disturbing story that I heard was from a 40-something woman. When she raised a LIFE question with her Internet date, it was easy to label this jerk. She asked, "What would you do if your wife got breast cancer?" His response knocked him out of the running for potential life partner immediately. Without feeling he answered, "I would leave her." When I shared this scenario with other men and women, everyone had a strong emotional reaction. One 42-year-old female commented, "I would have punched him in the face and run for the door."

- Lastly, I know a 26-year-old female Financial Advisor who had met a 38-year-old Acupuncturist online. They experienced an instant Chemistry Connection and the first date ended with a hug and nice kiss. She described her initial impressions of him to me: "He expressed a desire for a relationship, was very complimentary, and had good communication skills." She continued, "He was very sweet, articulate, kind-hearted, and very enthusiastic about connecting with me." He called her every day, and the relationship seemed to be progressing. The couple went out to dinner six weeks into the relationship and she "could feel that something was different." After dinner, he confessed his reservations to her about moving forward. She told me, "His guru told him that he should not be with me, so he broke it off." Another wacko bites the dust.

More Casual Chat Rooms

In addition to Internet dating sites, some people like to meet people through more casual internet chat rooms. Many of these rooms are oriented to specific topics or subjects so it may be easier to find someone with common interests in them. For example, one man I know meets women exclusively through chat rooms devoted to "health." He ascribes to healthy eating and living and so enjoys discussing the latest fads, supplements, and workout techniques.

The problem with chat rooms is you don't see a photograph of someone, though you can ask someone to email one to you privately. Nor can you search for someone with specific characteristics or interests or who lives in a desirable geographic location. In fact, I'd classify the man above as a perpetual emailer. He's happy to have pen pals all over the country so geographic location doesn't matter to him. My guess is that anyone who is serious about finding someone to date is using Internet matchmaking sites not chat rooms. I haven't used chat rooms myself, but my advice is to be cautious and use all the Net SMART Safety tips above for your own protection.

Chat rooms are not hopeless, but I would proceed with caution. During my research, I met a couple in their sixties who met in a chat room. The man was widowed and later met his second wife in a chat room where gardening tips were discussed. By following their instincts, they started a long-distance relationship that eventually led to a happy marriage. It is possible to find someone using a chat room, but it is definitely a more risky avenue.

Remember It's about Patience and Persistence so K.I.T.

Don't let the numbers game discourage you. It takes a lot of candidates to get down to four or five potential dates. At one point in my Man Hunt, I had received more than 400 email inquiries from four Internet dating sites. I actually decided to talk to twenty-five candidates on the phone. From this group of twenty-five, I arranged to meet twenty for coffee or drinks and then went out on second or third dates with five potential partners. With Internet dating, it's about patience and persistence. It may seem like a lot of work to weed through so many candidates, but it can be exciting and fun too. Just keep your sense of humor and adventure and remember to K.I.T. (Keep-it-Together).

Whatever happens during your dating journey, remember K.I.T. As a survival technique, use this as a mantra. It can help you keep your cool even when you are ready to scream or cry. Dating is not always easy, and you will find twists in the new era road, however, getting upset is a waste of energy and makes you much less attractive. Despite the dating hurdles you may encounter, you can succeed by keeping your positive attitude, a sense of humor and remember to just keep saying "Next" until you find man. It will happen. It is just a matter of numbers and time.

Enter the Widest Web Wrap Up

Connections made through the Internet and online matchmakers have many benefits. As an exercise, it is definitely a great ego boost and will increase your traffic flow giving you great "dating practice." You can find a high-quantity of men on the Internet, but need to carefully sort through the candidates. While I had some strange encounters, I did meet some attractive and intriguing candidates too. You'll make your Internet dating experience easier by heeding the advice in "Weeding through Email—The Net Selection Process" and "Net SMART Safety Tips." You'll also save yourself some time and trouble by benefiting from the wisdom of women who have gone before you when you use the SMART ABC Man Codes provided in Section IV.

Remember to be patient, persistent, and to continually work on expanding your home box. Oh, and don't forget your sense of humor since you will meet some real characters. When I got discouraged, I would remember all the Internet matchmaking success stories I've heard. I'd call my married friends from Arizona who met on the Internet and now live in Washington D.C. The husband would encourage me to keep trying. When I asked him what he found to be the biggest benefit of Internet dating, he told me, "You have access to people that you never would otherwise. A lot of people don't go to bars anymore so it is a great way to meet your man."

CHAPTER SIX

Test Quick Shot Dating

Do you want to know a Man Hunt shortcut? After weeks of Internet dating, a friend recommended that I try something new called Speed Dating or *Rapid Dating*. The idea provides a fast and effective way to get dates and seek a mate in the New Era.

This quick shot approach is the most time-efficient dating trend in the New Era. You sign up for an evening event where you meet ten to twenty candidates during introductory sessions of five to ten minutes each. These Speed Dating twirls are scheduled based on age ranges and can be a great way to quickly increase your bandwidth of potential suitors.

Five-Minute Men

During job interviews, most managers can tell whether they are interested in a candidate within minutes. Similarly, you can probably determine if you want to see someone again within the five to ten minute timeframe of these introductory dates. When I was Internet dating, in most cases when I first met a candidate in person, I knew within minutes whether I wanted to see him again. So this quick shot approach seems to make sense. It's a SMART way for men and women to go hunting for a mate. SMART Man Hunting is about getting out there, increasing your dating volume, boosting your ego by getting attention, and ultimately finding a great mate. Speed Dating is an excellent dating option for a busy woman in the 21st century.

How does Speed Dating work? While there are many groups offering this service to singles, the basic process follows.

Speed Dating Steps

1. Search the web for speed dating providers in your area.

2. Select a speed dating event and RSVP via the event provider's website.

3. Receive an email with the event address from the host.

4. Bring your smile, confidence, and a positive outlook to the event.

5. Meet men fast in five to ten minute interviews during the evening.

6. After each interview, write down the man's first name and circle "Yes" or "No" on a sheet to indicate if you want to meet him again.

7. Wait a day or two while the host determines whether any of the men you wanted to meet again want to meet you again too.

8. Receive an email from the host with your mutual matches and how to reach them.

9. Set up a meeting with your mutual matches as a next step.

SPEED DATING—A PERSONAL TALE

Speed Dating has been a positive experience for me; here is my tale with some additional insights. I first signed up for a *Rapid Dating* evening for 28 to 48 year olds in Santa Monica and it was really fun and time effective. Even though I was older than some of the men, I still came out with some great candidates in the end and maybe even a potential Mr. Right.

There were about fifty singles at this event. We met at a nice hotel bar and were given an evaluation sheet for the evening's activity. Similar to musical chairs, the event involves rotating places. The men were seated at numbered tables while the women moved to the next guy every five minutes when the bell rang. Our event host told us to simply write down each man's first name and then circle "Yes" or "No" after the five-minute introductory meeting.

Light-Hearted Approach: I decided to take a light-hearted approach and just go with the flow of the event. I started out the sessions by trying to be goal-oriented so I got to the point and asked each man for three things that he seeks in a mate. I found this question to be too complicated and serious for five-minute meetings, so I just started to relax and enjoy myself. Once I started using my KISS (Keep-it-Simple-Stupid) questions for first dates, the results were much better.

Some of the men actually had their own pointed questions for me. One asked me to tell him about the most "romantic place" that I had visited. I hesitated and then told him Santorini, Greece. Then he admitted, "That was actually a trick question because my most romantic place is anywhere with that special someone." I liked him.

Punchy Talk: By the time that I reached the tenth guy, everyone was getting punchy. At this point I found myself being side-tracked by my main mission and doing stuff like spending five minutes talking about the importance of names and how they can impact someone's ego. I think that I launched into this conversation because my brother was about to have a second baby and everyone was anxious to find out the new name.

By the end of the Speed Dating twirls, I had met twelve candidates and selected four as "Yes" men. The host explained that we would receive an email the next day listing the contact information (which is what you decide to share) for our matches if both parties marked "Yes."

The Rapid Results: The next day an email arrived with my matches. All four of my Yes men said yes to me. I trusted my gut, was selective, and contacted two of the men. While I found the first match extremely together and attractive during our follow-up coffee date, I was hesitant to date him because of our 12-year age difference. The second match blew me away. It turned out that I'd met him in passing earlier and he'd been thinking about contacting me again. In addition to this previous connection, our personalities seemed to click and I was definitely attracted to his "mojo." When it did not work out with this Mr. Click after three weeks of intensity, a wise friend reminded me, "If it sounds too good to be true, it probably is the case."

After a recovery timeout, I ended up back in two more sessions of *Rapid Dating* to test out their new age ranges of 25–40 and 35+years. I met more interesting men and made several business connections. The new age ranges worked well for me and both evenings were successes. I definitely recommend this type of New Era dating.

One night, I met two brothers and liked both of them. Brother # 1 had a candle and candy hearts on his table. Meanwhile, when I asked Brother # 2 what he was seeking in a mate, he told me: "I ask three questions: 1. Do they have a happy soul? 2. Does she like herself? and 3. Is she passionate and romantic?" Wow. Unfortunately, because they were brothers, I couldn't choose between them!

Advice for Speed Daters

- It's a good idea to review Section III, "The Dating Assessment Dance" before you leave home. Attend events with a positive and light-hearted attitude. People are attracted to an upbeat personality versus someone who is low energy—so give it your best shot by letting your personality shine!

- Go with low expectations so you can maintain your positive persona. It's a numbers game so you're bound to meet some people who make you turn green. But remember, it is only five minutes of pain. Chances are that you will make at least one connection in an evening.

- Take the pressure off yourself and just try to have some fun. You are there for the evening so relax and be yourself for the best results. I recommend that you use KISS (Keep-It-Simple-Stupid) questions and remember to ask yourself, "Would I ever want to kiss this person?" Ask him about his favorite vacation or what he likes to do for fun versus his resume.

- Dress for success! You don't need to dress for the ball, but wear something that makes you feel good and is "business casual" so no jeans or tennis shoes please!

- Be open to the idea of meeting new friends or business connections along with potential mates. You might set up follow-up meetings with people you meet during your Speed Dating adventure. You never know how they might help you or how you can help them in meeting dates or business contacts. For example, one evening I met a screenwriter who shared a similar passion for writing. He was working on a screenplay for the Sundance Film Festival at the same time that I was writing this book. I gained a great book cheerleader by attending Speed Dating. You might find supporters too.

Test Quick Shot Dating Wrap Up

Speed Dating is an excellent concept and is very time-effective. As one 30-something woman said to a group of us at a recent Speed Dating event, "I get more dates out of this type of thing than parties or bars." She added, "You've got to stir the pot. If you're not out there, nothing is going to happen." Search the Internet for an event near your home, and then ask them for references if you want a second opinion. Find out where the event will be held and go with an open mind. You might be punchy by the end of the evening after meeting so many men or find yourself pleasantly surprised that you made a connection or two.

CHAPTER SEVEN

Consider Using the Professionals

Beyond Internet dating and Speed Dating, New Era daters are also hiring Professional Matchmakers and attending professionally arranged singles events, both of which may involve a variety of approaches and different levels of intensity for finding a soul mate. You will need to determine what works best for you. Here are a few matchmaker options and personal insights from daters who have tried these services.

Serious Players

If you do not want to go the Internet dating route, there are several types of professional matchmaking services available that offer more thorough candidate screening for a price. While these services charge a much higher fee, you can eliminate some of the misrepresentations by men that go along with the dating game using this more structured approach. Professional Matchmakers can be a great choice if you are serious about your search and willing to make an investment in finding a high-quality Mr. Right. Check out different services and ask for references if you want to hear about their success stories.

Partnering with the Professionals

While Professional Matchmakers operate in ways that are similar to the Internet matchmaking sites there are differences. Here's how they work:

1. Set up an in-person meeting with a matchmaker's Service Coordinator to discuss their process and your goals.

2. Define your best attributes, along with what you desire in an ideal mate by completing statistic sheets and writing enticing personal essays.

3. Provide appealing and recent photographs that include a close-up and full-length hobby shot to let your personal attributes shine.

4. Partner with the matchmaker to narrow their pool of candidates by using your statistics and interests as a way to identify most-likely-to-succeed men.

5. And/Or wait until a guy picks you and let him make the first moves.

6. From this shorter list of candidates, take a closer look by reviewing their photos for a Chemistry Connection Test and personal essays.

7. Select a few good men and indicate interest in going on a first date. Let the guy or matchmaker make the plans and simply prepare your smile.

8. If the guy passes the Chemistry Connection Test on the first date, let him take the lead by setting up a second date.

9. If you decide to keep seeing him, do not stop dating until you hear, "I want you and only you," and the feeling is mutual.

TWO EXPERIENCES WITH PROFESSIONAL MATCHMAKERS

Do you want to learn more about this option? Here are two stories from women who tried the same professional matchmaking service with completely different goals and results.

Bachelorette # 1: This 37-year-old Operations Manager told me about her experience with a professional dating service. She paid a few thousand dollars versus the $25.00/month that many of the average Internet dating sites charge for their services. She kept it very quiet, and commented to me, "It was a last resort and I never wanted to admit that I was that desperate."

She was given an extensive packet to complete regarding her background and interests for her profile notebook. She also had a photo shoot with a professional photographer and placed these pictures in her personal profile as well. In addition, the service filmed videos of all candidates which were housed in a library for prospective dates to access. Once all of her personal data was gathered, she was assigned a reference number versus a name to protect her privacy. To view the folders of men, she had to physically visit the dating center. If my girlfriend was interested in learning more after reading someone's folder, she could view the potential date's video in the center. Once a candidate was identified, she could leave a reply card inquiry at the administration desk for the individual to pick up based on his ID number.

My girlfriend went out on a few dates but did not meet the man of her dreams. She found that both of her dates were more interested in talking about themselves and did not want to hear her point of view. In addition, her timing was wrong. She wasn't really ready to find a Mr. Right, but was only trying out the service to meet new people. It's not worth spending money on a professional matchmaker unless you are serious.

Bachelorette # 2: Alternatively, another woman who I interviewed used the same professional matchmaking service with marriage results. As a successful businesswoman, she applied her business savvy to her search, taking it very seriously. She told me, "I look for talent for a living. In my job, you might find one person in a hundred who fits a particular assignment—and that's probably good odds. I had just broken up with the wrong one soon after my 40th birthday and knew that I had to up my numbers."

Once this winning 40-year-old created her profile at the dating service, she received two hundred solicitations from men within six months. She had initially selected four men to approach, but later decided that she wanted men to contact her first. She actually went on dates with nineteen men, and wound up marrying one of the two hundred who had expressed interest in her.

How did she receive so many inquiries? Her advice to anyone setting up a profile with a dating service: "You have to be sincere, but also sound appealing. You have to find the right balance in your personal profile." She added, "I made every effort to make the pictures and video look good—I thought of it like a marketing tool, keeping in mind that the whole purpose is to attract men."

So what happened next? She shared more insights about her process with me: "I took it as seriously as finding a new job. I went to the dating center every week, checked who picked me, eliminated the definite No's, looked at videotapes, and then narrowed it down. I was picked by about fifteen men a week, I read their profiles, which usually led me to view seven videotapes, from there, I'd whittle it down to about four men who I'd be willing to meet in person."

As far as the dating process, she shared, "You kind of need to be brutal, but I wasn't interested in just dating." A few times after talking to them on the phone, she decided not to meet them. She also bumped into two "creepy guys." However, she ended up going on second dates with five men and married one of these five.

She also had a strict "no kissing" policy about until after a connection was made. While this approach may sound odd, her strategy was: "Women need to get themselves more in the driver's seat." She added, "My husband is the loveliest guy, but most men will try to get you in bed early. They will try and then take you for granted, and I wanted to avoid that situation."

Her Mr. Right was only six weeks older than her and it took five dates before she started having strong feelings for him. Initially, he did not call for a month between dates, so she just kept dating away. However, after a while they had a more relaxed, informal pool date where genuine connections were made. She added, "I was dating three guys at the time of the pool date and not kissing any of them." The happy couple dated for one year before getting engaged and married six months later.

She explained what she considered to be her top three advantages for using the dating service: "1. Because it is expensive, you have people that are a little more serious and it weeds out the riff raff. 2. I love it that you have access to so many people, 3. I liked the videotapes."

Lunch Men

Do you want someone else to do the homework? Do you have time for lunch? You might want to consider a matchmaker who schedules singles for lunch dates. This type of service may not be as expensive as some of the other Professional Matchmakers and seems like a good middle-ground option. The price may seem high, but it's not the highest. Similar to other Professional Matchmakers, the benefit is that candidates tend to be higher quality.

Most lunch men whom I met were busy professionals who wanted to meet women outside their office or client list. I paid an annual fee, which would guarantee me at least fourteen lunch dates per year and an average of one to two lunches per month.

The Lunch Dating Process

1. Meet with a Lunch Dating Coordinator

The first step is to find a lunch dating service. You can search for one in your area on the web. Next arrange to meet with the service's Dating Coordinator who interviews every candidate to document individual goals and desires in a relationship. The matchmaker takes your picture for their files, checks your license to make sure you are providing the correct age, and then goes to work setting you up with people whose preferences match your characteristics and desires.

2. Receive Your Man Candidates

The Dating Coordinator will call you with a list of candidates and will pitch them to you. You evaluate how someone sounds and whether you are willing to have lunch with him. If your interest is sparked, the Coordinator will work with both of you to set up a time and place for you to meet. You never have to contact the Man Candidate and he doesn't contact you so this process is much closer to a blind date.

3. Go to Lunch or Drinks

Meet your lunch man at a local restaurant for lunch or drinks (sometimes it is not a lunch date.) Again, take a light-hearted approach and do not take the date too seriously. This attitude helps reduce nerves on both parts and I have found it makes them want you more.

4. The Feedback Loop

After each date, both parties are encouraged to call the dating service to provide feedback on each lunch meeting. Obviously, the goal is to have satisfied clients and the feedback helps the service to ensure long-term success. It's a good idea to talk to the Coordinator after your lunch dates. By sharing with the Coordinator your likes and dislikes about a lunch date, it will help them find men closer to what you desire when setting up future dates.

5. Hold Option

A positive feature of some services such as lunch dating is that you can put the service "on hold." You might want to activate this option when you are already dating so many men that you can't handle any more. Or you may have met a Mr. Right and decided to date him exclusively for a while. If your Mr. Right or the other men you are dating don't make the final cut, you can always reactivate your membership in the lunch club.

6. Read the Fine Print

When signing up with any dating service, be sure to read the fine print and find out whether you can place your membership on hold and how it works. You will pay valuable money for Professional Matchmakers so be sure you understand the fine print. If you meet someone special, it is nice to know that you can stop the clock, and then pick up with the service later if your current Mr. Right candidate falls through.

Set Your Own Pace at Singles Events

Along with Professional Matchmakers, there are many singles groups out there that organize events with a theme. These organized activities can be a great way to get your feet wet in the New Era dating arena. All you need to do is find an event, show up with a smile, and then see if you catch anyone's attention. There is no pressure to perform one-on-one because you are not paired up. You set the pace, take what you want, and leave the rest behind.

Because you are only sharing basic personal information with the Event Coordinator when you sign-up, this is the safest route to meet people with the least amount of pressure. Simply search on the Internet for singles events near your home, find one with a theme that excites you, and then get out there and check it out. You might recruit a girlfriend to go with you to increase your comfort level, and then go have some fun with this dating option.

The themes of typical singles events are inviting and include everything from ski trips to Academy Awards parties. I found a broad range of singles events options out there including athletic activities, dinners, weekend adventures and even international travel. Here is a snapshot of some types of singles events:

Singles Event Themes

- St. Patrick's Day Party
- Academy Awards Party and Dinner
- Weekend Ski Trip
- Las Vegas Weekend
- Adventures in South America
- Water Ski Weekend
- Cruise the Seine
- New Orleans Jazz Festival
- Tennis Social

In addition to the types of events listed above, I discovered during my research, that singles dinners are cropping up around the country. I attended a few singles dinners that I found through an Internet date who turned out to be a friend versus a Mr. Right candidate. He recommended a dinner club organized by a woman who had recently moved back to Los Angeles from New York. Our party organizer was interested in meeting new singles and friends. She graciously opened her house for monthly dinners, and asked everyone to bring wine and new faces to broaden the circle.

These singles dinners included an equal number of men and women and often featured a theme. For example, one night we had a wine tasting where everyone brought their favorite Merlot. We rated the wines on score cards and the activity sparked great conversation amongst the crowd. Another evening, we invited an astrologer to share brief personality descriptions about the guests, and then everyone guessed who matched the profile.

Singles events can offer a variety of fun activities for meeting Man Candidates, but how successful can you be if it is a free-for-all mating scene? As in every New Era option that I researched, I came across success stories for singles events. My singles dinner organizer told me a story about a 39-year-old doctor who met her fiancé at a singles dinner. She became engaged to the 35-year-old retail entrepreneur after only ten months with the wedding planned for the fourteen month mark.

Since they are group activities rather than one-on-one interviews, singles events can take the pressure off, contribute to your numbers game, and significantly increase your chances of finding a man. If nothing else, you are not sitting home alone and should congratulate yourself for being brave and taking a chance. As a result, you might be surprised by how much fun you find and meet a Man Candidate simply by getting out there.

Consider Using the Professionals Wrap Up

Professional Matchmakers can be expensive, but the higher-quality of candidates may be worth it. If you are looking for professional men with money to burn, these services are right for you. Since the profile pool tends to be more professionals with more money, you can guess that the people who use these services will be somewhat older. Younger guys are still looking for women in bars, though not always. Be sure to ask the matchmaker the percentage of men versus women in your dating age range using their service. Professionals are also setting up lunch dates, singles dinners, and other group-based single activities. Try using these lower cost alternatives to Professional Matchmakers if you want to get out there and let someone else to do the work.

Chapter Eight

Expanding Your Home Box Part II

Hopefully, the whole time you're exploring the SMART Man Hunting landscape by trying on different New Era dating options, you've also heeded my advice in the first chapter of this section to continue to expand your Home Box. Not only will broadening your horizons make you more interesting to your friends and Man Candidates, but you'll be having a lot of fun and building confidence. At this point, I'd like to talk about some more developments in the New Era Man Hunting Landscape that you may not have considered.

Open Your Mind to International Flux

Global commerce and the worldwide web have made the world a pretty small place indeed. Have you ever met anyone from another country who opened your eyes to different perspectives? There is a flux of people traveling internationally today. Don't discount meeting men born in or living in other countries as potential dates or friends. Being more international in your outlook is a great way to expand you Home Box and broaden your overall perspective on life.

When I was living in Washington, D.C., I found myself meeting a variety of people from all over the world. I worked for a multinational organization, which made it easier to meet and maintain international contacts here and overseas. While you do not necessarily want to date your business contacts, you never know whom they might want you to meet and what knowing them might teach you. Most of the men I've met were nothing more than friends, but I met a few Man Candidates along my journey too.

Broaden Your World with International Travel

International travel is an ideal way to expand your Home Box so consider taking a trip abroad. Not only can it broaden your dating opportunities, but it will enhance your life skills. Travel calls forth any variety of skills and requires you to rise to a number of challenges. Dealing with people of different cultures is great practice for the interpersonal dance we do on the Man Hunt. By staying open while you travel, in addition to meeting potential partners, you'll develop lasting friendships. By asking questions, I learned about new cultures and built business connections that I keep today.

My approach was based on some good advice from my aunt. She told me, "Go as a traveler and not a tourist." Her advice was to focus on learning about a country's culture and values versus just joining the crowd and flocking to popular monuments. Because I took her advice to heart, the personal rewards and knowledge gained while traveling abroad were invaluable.

THE SAFARI STUD

On a business trip, I met a 35-year-old Lebanese Safari Guide while visiting Dubai, U.A.E. He totally opened my eyes to other outlooks on life and is one of the most positive and happy people that I have ever met. He immediately drew my attention when I first met him on a safari. He started the tour with this statement, "Tonight will be one of the most memorable nights of your life. You will see things that you have never seen before and always remember this tour." He also sparkled with a sense of humor. By clowning around with us, he made us laugh when our four-wheel vehicle got stuck in the sand dunes. A definite Man Candidate, he could barely buy me a cup of coffee, but his confidence and worldliness drew me to him.

During my first three-week visit to the U.A.E, we became inseparable. One night we sat on the beach and played what I called "20 questions" at the time (which is now part of the LIFE Match Game.) When I asked him to tell me about the scariest time of his life, he proceeded to describe how he almost died in a battle during his conscripted stint in the Lebanese army in his twenties. Dubai was his escape route. I had never met anyone in the United States with this type of story.

When I returned to Dubai five months later, I learned more from this international connection. I scheduled a safari for my training class, and the Safari Guide took us to a goat farmer's house during the excursion. We sat in the middle of the hot red-sand desert on rugs shielded from the sun by a canvas tent and sipped tea while attempting to communicate through non-verbal sign language with our hosts. Wow, simply by stepping out and setting up this safari, my worldly view was expanded with a new appreciation of western civilization!

He zest for life was irresistible. He shared that, "I have women all over the world who send me love letters and tell me that they want to have my children." I believe it. I often tease him about my code name for this female magnet, "Safari Stud." He continues to be my friend today despite the fact that he lives on the other side of the globe.

International Mr. Rights

Have you met any international Mr. Right candidates in your Man Hunt? Because the world has become a much smaller place, you are now more likely to meet a man who is from or lives in another country. One

47-year-old executive told me, "I met my girlfriend at a wedding. She lived in England, but has now moved back to Los Angeles."

In this small world, you never know whom you might meet. One of my Internet dating candidates emailed me, "I am in the South of France. I uploaded my pictures from Singapore. Will be in Los Angeles on Wednesday. Do you want to have coffee?" This email definitely caught my eye because I wanted to meet world travelers.

After speaking on the phone, I met this guy for coffee on a Saturday morning. He explained, "I'm in the process of moving back to Los Angeles from England." We shared many similar interests in both telecommunications and international business. During this meeting, I also discovered that he was a WD (Wounded Divorcé, see more SMART ABC Man Codes in Section IV.) He had just left his wife and it had been a tough good-bye. When I expressed my interest in getting re-married, he responded, "Does it have to be a marriage?" We parted as friends after three dates.

While that connection did not work, a 35-year-old woman from Tokyo, Japan, who recently moved to the United States to be with her man told me a success story. She had met her partner while working on World Cup events there. He was a U.S.-based photographer assigned to the World Cup while she was working in the medical center. She felt attracted to him, so, thinking fast, she asked him for guidance on how to best use her new expensive camera.

In order to take scenic shots and share her Japanese culture, she took him to visit a temple. She described their adventure and emotional connection, "We went to a small stone temple where memorial stones are placed by women who have lost babies. Once he learned about this tradition, his mood changed. I found out that he had lost a baby many years ago. He wanted to place a stone in honor of his child in the temple.

He started crying and decided to buy a stone. She said, from that moment forward, "I knew that I could trust his heart."

After the 57-year-old photographer left Japan, the couple talked on the phone several times a day, often for hours at a time. She said to me with a grin, "We spent a lot of money on the telephone." After two failed arranged-marriage attempts by her mother earlier in Japan, she flew the coop and has landed with her new man in America.

Don't Discount Long Distance

The key thing to remember about International Mr. Rights is that it's a small world. Don't be so quick to eliminate a candidate from overseas. If you meet someone you cannot resist, it is easier now in the New Era than at any other time to entertain long distance dances with an International Man.

The same holds true for men who live in the same country as you but maybe not in your city. Thanks to telecommunications, you are no longer limited by geography in the New Era so that long-distance romances are more feasible.

If you meet someone via email introductions, Internet dating, matchmakers or business travel, distance is no longer an insurmountable hurdle. As one wise 60-something man told me, "If you hit it off, there is no such thing as 'Geographically Undesirable' anymore." While meeting someone outside the city walls may not be ideal, modern technology makes it easier today to maintain a relationship.

Long Distance Quality Time

The biggest hurtle in long distance relationships is to find ways to maintain intimacy and time. There are cheap and easy ways to maintain regular communication today with a long-distance partner. You always have the email option, which is free and eliminates time zone difference considerations. I have also found that cell phones and calling cards minimize long-distance bills. These options can reduce the stress of talk-time limits and lessen the financial burden. Don't forget about pagers, personal organizers and text messages as alternative ways to maintain long distance communications with your mate.

In addition to benefiting from communications technology, it's still important to have quality face time with each other. Luckily, flying to meet a long-distance partner for quality time together is no longer an obstacle. You can make a long distance relationship work well when one partner flies to the other's city on a monthly basis. Despite the delays due to increased security measures at airports, discount fares and multiple flights make it practical to visit your mate on a regular basis.

One 30-something male explained his long-distance relationship to me. He said, "She works as a consultant so we alternate weekends. I fly to her once a month, and then she comes here another weekend." After two years of dating long distance, the dynamics of the long distance dance have worked for them. Not only is the couple committed to each other, but they share similar cultural backgrounds. Both parties are Chinese and grew up in Australia. Because their foundation is so solid and there is a genuine respect for each other, they can handle any relationship distance hurdles. These Winning Long Distance Dancers are now engaged after surviving a consulting assignment that separated the couple between Rome and Los Angeles for six months.

DOS AND DON'TS FOR LONG DISTANCE

Do's	Don'ts
Give long distance love a try if there is a strong mutual connection and both parties are committed to give it a go.	Don't waste your time with men who are not serious contenders. Unless the guy is communicating his feelings and making plans to see you again, he is not in this long-distance game.
Use modern technology to build the bond and sparks through regular communications.	Avoid big long distance bills by using cell phones, calling cards, email, and text messages for communications.
Make an effort to meet at least once a month in person to allow for quality time and to keep the relationship moving forward.	Don't let yourself get so busy that you can't find time to meet. You might drag out a relationship for months or even years without having regular contact only to find out he is Mr. Wrong.
Periodically give yourself a reality check about the relationship and make a go/no go decision.	If the guy is not talking about the future after a few months, stop dreaming about what might happen and cut your losses.
Build your own network before making a move for a man so you don't lose your confidence sex appeal.	Never make a move only for the guy. You only want to move if the new location complements your needs.

Making a Long Distance Move Decision

At a certain point, you need to have a discussion about whether someone should move so that you can be together. The globetrotting will get
old and, eventually, you will need to make a go/no-go decision. Set a
time limit for making this decision and then periodically monitor your
progress. During the long-distance courtship, encourage an on-going
dialogue so you understand each other's expectations.

Moving is a serious milestone and making a move demonstrates a serious commitment. Consider what the new location brings to you as an
individual versus moving only for your partner. For women, careers,
interests, and friends bring balance to a relationship. Losing these sup-
ports can put undue pressure on a personal connection. Start building a
support network prior to making a move. My relocation to Los Angeles
from Washington D.C., was prompted, in part, by a long distance relationship. As soon as I first entertained the idea of a West Coast move, I
immediately started building other connections out there through high
school friends, college connections, and work friends. I found a new job
using the Internet and acquaintances, re-connected with a childhood
friend living in Los Angeles, and rented my own apartment in Santa
Monica. I wasn't about to put all my eggs in my suitor's basket. I was
personally ready for a change in geography for many reasons, not just
for the man.

And it was a good thing that I took this "build your foundation first"
approach, because once I moved, I quickly learned that my partner was
at a stage where he could not handle a relationship in the same city. I
was able to adjust quickly and accept that he was not emotionally ready
for a commitment. Because I had already built my support systems, I
was able to move on more easily.

This story brings up one of the downsides to long distance relationships.
They might work only because they are long distance. In other words,

you and your man may both be busy professionals who don't have time for more than a phone friend and twice-a-month weekend date. When you do get together, there might be too much pressure to fulfill a fantasy and reality gets diluted. In fact, someone who regularly gets involved in long distance romances may not be ready to commit to more than that, like my man friend above.

You don't ever want to move because you think a man is going to fix your life. You need balance to keep your confidence and sex appeal. Always try to keep your interests in mind first when making a move inspired by a long distance partner. In the end, you will have a more fulfilling life and be a better partner. The moral of the story: Keep your Home Box open and keep expanding its boundaries.

Expand Your Home Box II Wrap Up

There are enough long distance dating success stories including international ones to encourage you to stay open to Man Candidates from other countries or cities. It's a global economy these days and that includes the New Era dating options. The key is to be willing to continually expand your Home Box and try different experiences and dating options.

Exploring the New Era of Man Hunting— Start Dating up a Storm

With this baseline understanding of New Era dating mechanics and opportunities and armed with safety guidelines, you can begin taking advantage of all the expanded dating options to start dating up a storm. These new trends and tools provide multiple angles for success in the 21st century dating game.

- These modern dating scene themes create endless possibilities for finding your man.

- Email is a blind date enabler and provides a great way to flirt with your man.

- Internet Dating is more accepted, provides the most Man Candidates, and can boost your ego by the increased dating activity.

- Chat rooms and singles events allow you to set the dating pace and share similar interests.

- Speed Dating produces the fastest results in least amount of time.

- Professional Matchmakers can provide more help and higher quality candidates.

- International mixing can open your eyes to new cultures and Man Candidates.

- Long-distance romance is now more feasible with 21st century technologies.

With all the Man Candidates you're going to find yourself with, your biggest problem now is how to assess and evaluate them. The next section of this book provides you with everything you need for the Dating Assessment Dance—including GUT Instinct Checks, First Date Tests, Quick Qualifiers, and the LIFE Match Game—to help you identify your Mr. Right. In short, you will learn how to get the facts to assess your man and how to work with your own instincts to pick the best Man Candidate for you. Using these assessment tools, you can gain insights on ways to be selective versus settling for a nice guy who shows interest. Nice guys are not always a Mr. Right so don't settle for just anyone who adores you. Remember, searching for a life partner is equivalent to mining for gold. You want the gold, don't you?

SECTION III

The Dating Assessment Dance
Steps to the Perfect Match

CHAPTER NINE

What You Should Know Before You Go

Do you want to save time by learning from other people's successes and mistakes? Are you willing to review your Mr. Right candidates thoroughly for the best long-term results? Do wish to avoid the kind of failures you've experienced before in relationships?

Finding a lifetime man should be taken as seriously as searching for the right job. In this section, you'll learn how best to assess your man for the greatest assurance of long-term success. Remember a MAN Hunt is like a JOB Hunt. In fact, Mr. Right interviews are even more important than finding the most desirable job because a marriage deal is much harder to break.

SMART Man Hunting is all about making the right choice at the right pace based on the broadest range of options:

- SMART is proactively dating to expand your bandwidth to increase your odds.

- SMART is realizing that choosing a partner is one of the most important decisions you can make and it's important to be selective.

- SMART is making a commitment to yourself to fully evaluate every Man Candidate based on whether *he* fits *your* needs, interests, values, and long-term goals.

- SMART means asking the right questions, listening for the red flag clues, and then taking the time to observe his behavior to see whether he is a good match.

- SMART is about reality checks and knowing when to cut your losses and move on.

- SMART means pacing yourself and the relationship so as to enjoy the dating dance versus forcing it.

- SMART is about maintaining your confidence and sense of self as the relationship builds.

- SMART is knowing how to identify Mr. Right versus Mr. Right Now.

- And before you start your evaluation, remember SMART is patient and persistent versus desperate, so take your time, have fun, and avoid giving off needy vibes.

It's imperative that you avoid being swept into a relationship based primarily on hormones and make a conscious decision to evaluate the entire package. Not only will this spare you a lot of wasted effort and energy, but it's also apt to spare your feelings as well. Don't waste any more time on Mr. Wrongs. Instead devote your energy to finding Mr. Right, even if it takes some time.

How do you go about evaluating your Man Candidates? Maybe you've never even thought about it before because you've been more concerned about how *they* are evaluating *you*. Believe me they are. But forget about that for now. This Man Hunt is about what you want. This is about being SMART.

Man Candidate Interview Practices

So, you've entered the New Era, tried on all its dating options, and the men are lined up at your door. It's time to be selective. By properly interviewing and evaluating your Mr. Right candidates, you can succeed at a long-term relationship by taking the time to talk through your goals, interests and backgrounds with potential matches.

Your job is to evaluate which Man Candidates will stick. Whom do you want to see after your first date? Whom do you want to see for a second or third date? And then after the third date turning point, who is showing long-term or even marriage potential?

A wise 39-year-old film editor told me, "Dating interviews are all about testing flexibility and negotiating boundaries." By the time you get to the third date, asking LIFE Match Questions, active listening, and observing behavior can help you discover the real Man behind the Candidate to assess marriage potential. The film editor added: "You need to find out if the person is too extreme for you in certain areas." For example, if someone is a baseball fanatic and you have no interest in that sport, start asking questions to find out the importance to him of whether his partner joins him at all the games.

Dating assessment is a three step dance, one that you are doing with your date. While he's dancing, you're going to be dancing too. Each step is geared to a deepening level of interest in your date as you are opening up with each other. The steps are also about getting the information you need and recognizing red flags early so that you can make some decisions in the shortest period of time. Why spend months dating someone only to discover he's not right for you? With the Dating Assessment Dance Steps provided in this section, you'll be able to make a decision quickly—usually within the first three to seven dates. Try these steps to secure a long and happy relationship.

Mining for Mr. Right Gold

You can't mine for gold if you don't know what it is. In other words, what does Mr. Right look like to you? Before you even engage in Man Candidate Interview Practices, you have to know what you are looking for in a Perfect Match. Employers don't seek to fill a position without a job description, neither should you.

- *Identify your Key Criteria* What's your gold? Ask yourself what qualities and attributes you want to see in a lifetime man and consider how important they are to you. Qualities may include honesty, kindness, consideration, intelligence, approach to life, looks—in short, it's any variety of things. (If you need ideas, you can read more about how others define their Perfect Match at the end of this section.)

- *Define your Best Attributes* What's golden about you? Be able to define your best attributes, along with what you desire in a mate. Take a closer look at your behavior patterns and desires. Search for men who are seeking your best qualities for greater LIFE Match Game success. While you never want to try to become what someone is looking for, you'll have greater success if you are honest enough to know whether who you are fits what someone is telling you they want. If a man is looking for a great cook and take-out is your middle name, it's reasonable to assume that a match between you won't work. And if he asks you to describe yourself, you want to make sure you have your marketing pitch down. Remember you want someone to think of you as their gold.

Keep your Key Criteria in mind during all initial contacts with Man Candidates, whether in email, on the phone, or in person. Be prepared to eliminate anyone who doesn't fit the list. Once you mine for gold in the crowd, your chances of finding Mr. Right will rise significantly. By only meeting the top men, you will have a greater chance of finding a soul mate faster. If you are looking for a long-term relationship, don't waste time with unlikely matches. The opportunity cost is too high and you need to focus your energies on real candidates.

It is important not to force a match if there are major differences. If you identify someone that sounds great, but your key criteria do not complement each other, move on quickly to the next prospect. One 33-year-old Financial Manager shared this observation, "If you want to believe something, you can believe almost anything. People get lost in relationships and are not objective." You need to be truthful with yourself and objective on the Hunt.

Let Your GUT Be Your Guide

Have you ever noticed how often your friends end up dating or marrying men unlike any of the other men they've ever been with before? Or how often the people you know end up with someone you'd never have expected to see them with? How did that happen? What drew her to that man? I'm not talking about the disasters you can see from a mile away here, but the healthy, yet surprising, relationships around you.

The answer is probably the bottom line GUT factor. There is truth to the common wisdom, "Trust Your Gut." What is your gut telling you about a man. In SMART Man Hunting, your GUT should be alerting you to a potential Mr. Right even if "on paper" he's not what you initially might have been looking for. What is GUT? Try this expanded definition to look beyond the surface:

G   Genuine—Is he is real?

U   Understanding—Does he sincerely listen, care, and share his feelings with you?

T   Trustworthy—Is he trustworthy, reliable and of good character?

Much of this GUT definition is probably on your list of Key Criteria above. Everyone is seeking the same core GUT qualities in a life partner: honesty, trust, companionship, good communication, compromise, consideration, confidence and fun.

So why is it so hard to find? Timing and desire are probably the biggest hurdles. You need to find someone who is ready, willing, and able to share these core qualities with you. If you find a man who wants to expose his core with you topped by a Chemistry Connection, the wedding bells will be much closer than spending time with a candidate who builds fences around himself.

In SMART Man Hunting, it's important to let your GUT be your guide throughout your dating travels. If you're looking for a life partner, you're looking for GUT.

As my close 37-year-old girlfriend prepares for her wedding she told me, "It really matters what you feel when you're with the person. I like who I am when I am with him." She reconnected with a college friend after years of no contact. He was studying to be a minister and planning to visit India. Because my girlfriend had studied in India, he called her unexpectedly in Washington, D.C., from Texas to ask for advice.

After several calls and emails, they decided to visit in person. Within three months, she knew that he was "the one" for her. Her 37-year-old male partner is now moving to Washington, D.C., and has decided not to be ordained. The couple was open-minded about long-distance relationships, listened to their gut instincts, and found life partnership in the end.

One 45-year-old male CEO friend commented to me, "I see people all the time at parties with guys that don't look like the person you would expect them to marry. It's the same answer every time when I ask them why this guy? They tell me it is because he considers her feelings before his own." When you find someone who is GUT—genuine, understanding and trustworthy—you might just throw your Mr. Perfect checklist in the trash.

GUT Instinct Questions

Start checking your GUT with man candidates by asking yourself these questions:

- Is he real?

- Does he make me feel really good about myself?

- Is he enthusiastic about getting to know me?

- Is he polite and considerate to me and others?

- Does he share his feelings with me?

- Is he trustworthy?

- Is he reliable?

- Does conversation with him flow or is it a struggle?

- Can we share laughs together?

- Does he make me smile?

Take a closer look at the dynamics of the dance with your Mr. Right candidates. Besides asking them questions, you can learn a great deal simply by observing them. Remember the adage, "Actions speak louder than words." What is his behavior telling you? And as a wise 34-year-old female Marketing Manager told me, "If people contradict themselves with their behavior, pointing it out seems pointless. They're only telling you what you want to hear—been there, done that!"

Along with the basic GUT instincts, below are some observation clues. Men often express love and caring more freely through their actions than their words so watch for these good GUT signs and recognize the unspoken messages when identifying Mr. Right candidates early.

GOOD GUT MAN BEHAVIORS

Good GUT Man Action	The Unspoken Message
The guy is always on time or calls if he is running a little late.	He values and respects your time.
He opens the car door and pulls the chair back for you at restaurants.	He is a gentleman. He wants to show you consideration. There is no need for chivalry to be dead in the 21st century. Let him treat you like a princess.
The guy turns his cell phone off when he is on a date with you.	This man wants to be with you and only you during dates.
During the initial dance, he picks you up at your place and makes formal plans.	He wants to make an effort and treat you with respect.
The man is willing to compromise on how and when you meet and what you do together.	This guy is flexible, which is a great foundation for any relationship.
Your date gives you compliments, but does not go overboard.	He likes you.
He tells you about friends and family that he wants you to meet.	He wants to share his life with you, which is a great Mr. Right sign.

You might be surprised by the twists in your Man Hunt road. If the GUT is good with a man you would normally not consider, give him a second look.

Looking Beyond GUT

If you've got GUT, you also want to look beyond GUT. GUT can take you a long way, but you still need to be compatible in core areas and want the same things out of life and love. Even with GUT, you have to be SMART. So engage in all the SMART Man Hunting Interview Practices, Strategies, and the LIFE Match Game to see if your Good GUT Man can become a Mr. Right.

Give Him Three Chances to Enter the Mr. Right Lane

I recommend three dates before knocking someone off your Mr. Right Lane list if he passes the First Date Tests and looks like he could be a good GUT Man. By the third encounter, you'll have gathered enough information to make a solid assessment of the candidate. When you are seeking a new job, employers rarely offer the position on the first interview. In a similar manner, give the guy three chances to show his true colors, and then continue to monitor for reality checks and red flags as you move on to the LIFE Match Game.

Consider the Importance of LIFE Match

As you evaluate your Man Candidates, one of your main objectives is to test if your life goals, values and attitudes match up. One of the reasons so many couples may be divorcing these days is a failure to consider LIFE Match during courtship. LIFE Match is more than just statements of what you want or are seeking. It's all in the attitudes and actions.

LIFE Match will show you whether you and your Man Candidate have what it takes to go the distance.

What You Should Know Before You Go Wrap Up

You're ready to meet your Man Candidates and begin the Dating Assessment Dance. Before you go, it's a good idea to review your key criteria in a man and define what you think is "golden" about you. You know that finding a Mr. Right is about successful interview practices, listening for clues, and SMART observations so pack these skills in your bag. As a prelude to your Chemistry Connection, Quick Qualifiers, and the other early tests to see if your date has the potential to be a Mr. Right, you're reminded about the importance of good GUT. Is he Genuine, Understanding, and Trustworthy?

CHAPTER TEN

The Dating Assessment Dance—Step One Chemistry Connection and Coffee Talk

By now you've weeded out the undesirables, you've given some thought to what really matters to you, and have a few interested men in line. Are you ready to meet your Man Candidates? Do you like coffee? Even if you don't, find a coffee shop near your home, order something else, and then prepare for your first date questions and tests. The coffee shop is the ideal setting because it is a neutral, safe and public place. The first date is simply about testing the waters and building rapport. Relax, take a deep breath, put on your confidence, and avoid first date discussion bloopers. Focus on the following Chemistry Connection Test and KISS Questions in order to maximize results and minimize first date disasters.

Chemistry Connection Test

Ask yourself, "Do I want to kiss this guy?" A 48-year-old personal trainer told me that after a few email exchanges with Internet dating candidates, he often writes, "Don't you think it's time for us to meet at the coffee shop and decide whether we would want to kiss each other?"

As simple as that, this is the Chemistry Connection Test and it should be your primary objective on your first encounter with someone. One 39-year-old movie producer told me, "My friends have a 60-second test. They decide whether there is any chemistry within the first minute."

You might want to give the candidate a full hour before making a chemistry decision—especially if there's good GUT—even though you will probably know in the first five minutes.

Watch the non-verbal communication between you and the Man Candidate during the first date to guess how he rates you on his Chemistry Connection Test. A 35-year-old Paralegal Manager reminded me, "When identifying Mr. Right, the number one thing to consider is whether there is mutual sexual attraction." While you will probably know if there is a mutual attraction right away, observe his chemistry clues while remaining conscious of your own signals to him. Remember to be SMART, Sexy, and Confident. Similar to dressing for a successful job interview, wear something that makes you look and feel good. Your dress and positive persona will make lasting impressions on a man candidate. As one 47-year-old bachelor said to me: "Don't dress like you want to go to bed with the guy either." Instead, dress SMART for the occasion and draw him in with confidence versus skin.

Non-verbal Chemistry Connection Clues

Here are some non-verbal clue questions to keep in your purse for gauging the man's response on the Chemistry Connection Test:

- Is he smiling at you often?

- Is he leaning towards you?

- Is he nodding his head when you are making a point?

- Is he making direct eye contact or are his eyes wandering around the room?

- Does he try to make contact by reaching out to hold your hand or touch your shoulder?

- Does he raise his eyebrows to show enthusiasm when making important points?

- Does he open the door for you?

- Does he try to hug you good-bye?

- Does he try to kiss you when he says good-bye? (I'm okay with this move on a first date if there is a good connection. You need to decide your own boundaries.)

- Is he dressed nicely, or does he look like someone who just rolled out of bed? (Actually this isn't a Chemistry Connection Clue but a clue that this guy isn't all that interested. Next.)

If these non-verbal clues are present on a first date, they are great indicators of a physical attraction for and sincere interest in you. If you find the candidate physically appealing, give him the same type of positive confirmations in return. Because chemistry is a major part of the equation and up to eighty percent of communication is non-verbal, don't overlook the importance of this initial Chemistry Connection Test exchange.

KISS Approach

While the main point of the first encounter, testing to see if there is a Chemistry Connection, involves a non-verbal exchange, you're also going to have to do some talking. Approach your first dates with a very casual and relaxed attitude for the best results. When engaging in conversation, follow this wise KISS approach, "Keep it Simple, Stupid." Your only concern is whether you would consider kissing the candidate in the future.

Do not propose marriage on a first date. Never put a guy on trial. While you might be laughing, my Lunch Dating Coordinator told me, "I know women who have gotten very aggressive on their first date. The feedback was not good." You do not need to conduct a federal investigation on the first date. You want to be SMART about these meetings, and SMART is not desperate or aggressive, so relax.

Use easy and non-threatening questions during your first date to create a comfortable conversation. You are meeting a stranger, so simply take the opportunity to build rapport.

KISS Questions

Here is a short list of KISS questions that you can use during this brief first date meeting to keep things light and positive:

- What do you like to do for fun?

- How long have you lived here?

- Where did you grow up?

- What was your favorite vacation?

- Where would you like to visit if you could go anywhere in the world?

- Have you seen any good movies lately?

- What do you think the weather will do today? (A great KISS question for most of the U.S., but not as effective for Southern California—sorry to rub it in, but people don't talk weather that often in L.A.)

KISS Question Warning: Do not ask, "How is your dating going?" I cannot count how many men asked me, "How do you like Internet dating?" or "Have you had any success using Speed Dating?" during first encounters. These questions only bring up discussions about other dates and you are trying to avoid First Date Disasters.

Avoiding First Date Disasters

The number one cause of first date disasters is fear, which leads to discussion bloopers and unnecessary anxiety. Remember, you have adopted a No-Fear Attitude so you can avoid these clashes on your Man Hunt journey.

What fuels fear on first dates is either the fear of surprise, rejection or disappointment—and usually it's a combination of all three. I also think a primary cause of first date jitters is societal pressure to be successful. People tend to base self-worth on success in career and family. On first dates, there is extra conversational emphasis on these two areas since most first date questions always revolve around what you do for a living and what your relationship history might be. These questions come dangerously close to pressing low-self-worth buttons.

You need to forget about this pressure for an hour, relax, and focus on being positive. So what topics should you avoid discussing on a first date? Similar to the Internet dating tips discussed earlier, you want to hold your cards close to your chest. And don't share your whole life story. You are in marketing pitch mode so why bring up any dating obstacles?

First Date Discussion Bloopers

Do you want to avoid being added to the First Date Discussion Bloopers Hall-of-Shame? Then avoid getting too personal on first dates. Remember, the keys to success are the Chemistry Connection Test and KISS Approach. Here are three of my favorite bloopers that you should dodge on first dates:

- *Don't Bring Up Finances or Big Check Books* No one needs to know your financial status on a first date. Nor do they need to try to be impressed by fancy cars and big check books. A woman raised a question at one of my book signings regarding finances, she said, "I am living on disability payments. Do you think that I should tell this to a man on the first date because I want to be honest?" My response: "I believe in honesty, but don't bring it up on the first date. You need to decide whether you want to kiss him before you start sharing anything too personal." First dates are all about chemistry and that has nothing to do with material things. If you talk too much about finances on a first date, you will definitely kill the sparks.

- *Why Talk about Weaknesses?* Would you ever bring up your weaknesses in a job interview? Why would you ever share your scars during a first date? If you are having trouble dating, don't share that information with a date. You want to be Sexy, Smart, and Confident instead. I had drinks with a guy who told me on a first date, "Liz, I just can't figure out dating. I can't get women to call me back and they cancel plans with me at the last minute all the time." Why would he ever share this information with me on a first date? What a turn-off! This is too much information. Next.

- *Leave the Exes in the Car* Talking about past relationships is the number one mistake people make on first dates. I think daters feel self-conscious and want to clarify why they are no longer dating someone. I went out with a guy who told me on a first date that he left his wife, then got her pregnant, went back to have the baby, and was in the process of divorcing her again— Check Please! Why bother bringing any negative energy into the equation? You are both single now and on even ground. You want to be beaming with positive energy and make someone feel special so leave the ex in the car for the first few dates. And if you get asked about your ex, just give a nonchalant, casual response and then switch gears fast!

Always accent the positive because the first date is all about marketing yourself to a potential mate.

WHAT MEN WATCH IN WOMEN ON FIRST DATES

While I received many male comments about first dates, here is an insightful list from a 35-year-old-lawyer regarding what he watches in women on first dates.

- How does she carry herself?
- Is she wearing nice clothes that go together? Are her shoes worn out?
- Is she interested and receptive in me?
- Can she get my sense of humor?
- Can she maintain prolonged eye contact?
- Does she smile often? Does she smile and then look away with her eyes in a flirtatious way?
- Is she ok with showing some emotion that she likes me?
- Is she conversational or confrontational?
- Is she nodding to show that she is listening?

His bottom line comment about his observations, "I think a woman who carries herself well is ten times more attractive."

Remember, you want to highlight your strong points (and without being too boastful.) First conversations are about using the right balance to present a desirable package. It's not the words so much that matter, it's your attitude. SMART daters avoid dating disasters!

The Second Date Hunch

If the candidate has passed go on Chemistry Connection and it seems you've passed his test as well, you can expect that you'll be proceeding to the next date. If this doesn't happen, don't sweat it. Remember there are plenty of other men out there. Above all else, don't take it personally. There could be a thousand reasons why he doesn't want to see you again and usually none of them have anything to do with you. Anyway, if you misread the non-verbal clues and he felt no Chemistry Connection with you, who cares? Give yourself credit for putting your best foot forward and taking a chance. There will be plenty of men who will feel a mutual Chemistry Connection with you. Nothing's personal.

RED FLAG MEN

From the first step of your Dating Assessment Dance, you should be on the look-out for Red Flag Men. Usually you can only identify these guys in person, but once you do, you will know. Even when there is a Chemistry Connection, Red Flag Men should be avoided at all costs. The Chemistry Connection can blind you to who they are which is why I include them here.

This step is where you really need to rely on your GUT so listen to your instincts and if something does not feel good, get out fast. In order to save you time, embarrassment, and, possibly, heartache, I want to help you recognize these bad eggs. These tales may also bring you a sigh of relief when you realize that you are not alone if you have bumped into these guys in the past. Here are three types of Red Flag Men and the warning signs to look for on your Man Hunt journey:

Sly Schemer

The Sly Schemer is a "player." He is acting a part and will try to deceive you. This guy plays a game using either fancy words or material things to draw you into the bedroom as fast as possible. You need to watch out for the signs early and run for the hills. These actors will tell you whatever you want to hear to get you in bed. They are likely to be playing the game with multiple women at once as well. Watch out for men who give you too many compliments too early. Watch out for the guys with false promises.

In addition to playing with words, a Sly Schemer might shower you with gifts and take you to fancy restaurants for the sole purpose of winning you over so that you will sleep with him quickly. Unfortunately, many men follow a third date rule. If you are not in the bedroom with them by the third date, they disappear. They have found women who let them get away with it, so if they don't get what they want from you, they just keep moving until someone else falls for their antics. If a guy tries to impress you with material things right off the bat, take a closer look. Fancy dinners, flowers, and gifts should not lure you in too fast.

While dream men exist, beware of the guys who give too much too fast. I met a man through Speed Dating who ended up being a Sly Schemer. He took me to a five-star restaurant on the beach for the first date, brought me flowers on the second date and took me to a nice Italian restaurant, and then showed up on the third date with a thoughtful book. During this dating dance, he often called me in the middle of the day and said, "Are you thinking about me because I can't stop thinking about you?"

Because this guy just started sounding too good to be true, my GUT instincts started to whisper to me. When he asked me to take a shower with him on the third date, I knew that he was a short-timer versus someone interested in going the distance. I said no to this invitation and then never heard from him again, I knew this guy was just another Sly Schemer and my initial feelings were right on the mark. Watch out for men who come after you like a fast freight train filled with goodies and compliments at lightning speeds. They are not real deals. If it's Mr. Right you are trying to find, jump off this Mr. Wrong train immediately.

Macho Mind

The Macho Mind is a man who places men first, including male friendships, opinions, and activities. These men consider women more as sex objects than as life partners. He prefers spending time on the golf course with his buddies versus taking you away for a romantic weekend. You know these men. They will hang out with the guys over you any day. They place a greater value on hunting, playing poker, and watching football with the gang versus spending quality time with you. Macho Minds don't have female friends so they don't know what they are missing. So when you ask a guy, "What do you like to do for fun?" on a first date, watch for the clues in their answer to see if they have Macho Mind tendencies.

In addition, Macho Mind men don't get that when they are out with you they are not supposed to be checking out other women. A great red flag for Macho Minds is that even on the first date their eyes will be wandering to the other women in the room. He should be focused on learning about you versus staring at other women. I don't care if he is cute. If he does not give you his full attention on a first date, forget about him!

While I don't believe couples should have to share every activity and do think that each person should have their own friends, what's wrong with the Macho Mind is the attitude. These guys don't value women or their opinions or ideas, in fact, they don't even *like* being with women. I briefly dated a Macho Mind who told me, "I really value my male friends because we are going through many of the same things and we can talk about our careers." Excuse me? Don't women have careers these days? Valuing a female's opinion is not part of the Macho Mindset. What are these guys thinking? We are in the 21st century and to think that some men don't value what a woman thinks is mind-boggling and scary. You want to find someone who wants to hear your input on important decisions. Why waste time with Macho Minds?

Me-First Man

The Me-First Man is not always easy to recognize initially. This man is totally self-absorbed and pre-occupied with his accomplishments, career, work-out routine, and anything else that has to do with feeding his ego. Because the natural tendency is to swap resumes during the first few dates, it might be harder to identify the Me-First Man.

Look for clues when he discusses his schedule. Since he just met you, you can't judge him on how he fits you into his time, but what about his family and friends? Does he try to make an effort to make plans with others or does he just wait for the world to please him? Does he ever talk about spending time with the important people in his life? When he shares these encounters, does he describe them in terms only of himself and his needs? Is he set in his ways and his schedule to the point of rigidity? For example, does he need to work out every day at a certain time or he turns into a wild animal?

One of my girlfriends dated a 29-year-old man who was completely self-absorbed. He was fortunate to have grown up in a very affluent family and was handed all the nice things in life way too easily. This Me-First Man stuck to his daily work-out schedule at the club across the street, loved playing with his fancy cars, made her drive to his place all the time, and then rarely took time to listen to her interests and needs. When she jokingly commented to him one day, "You are spoiled rotten," he responded by saying, "You don't know the half of it." And if you think this statement is telling, listen to what he pulled on Valentine's Day. Not only did he show up empty-handed two months into the relationship, he didn't even take the time to make a dinner reservation. The couple ended up at a sushi bar and it made her feel horrible to be so taken for granted. Soon after receiving this Me-First message, she got smart and said, Next!

If a guy is so self-absorbed that he can't be bothered to listen to you talk about your day or buy you a card on Valentine's Day, what are you doing hanging out with this Me-First Man? Any time you run across this type of Red Flag Man, promptly hit the eject button. There is no give-and-take with these guys so where's the relationship potential?

The Dating Assessment Dance—Step One Wrap-Up

Congratulations, you made it past the first date and Coffee Talk. You made small talk while you were assessing the Chemistry Connection with your Man Candidate and observing his non-verbal cues about his attraction to you. This fun phase is about marketing, eliminating the obvious "Nos" and enjoying a bit of an adventure. And as one 31-year-old male, who is a Financial Manager, told me, "You are lucky to learn a little about the person on a first date."

Another active dater, a 42-year-old Production Coordinator, shared a similar perspective. She said, "It's basically a look and see. It's a show and tell." So go to first dates with low expectations, play it safe, bring your marketing pitch and try to have some fun versus fright. Now that you have knocked out the Red Flag Men and selected a few good candidates who you want to kiss, you're ready to roll up your sleeves and really suss out what makes your candidate tick.

CHAPTER ELEVEN

The Dating Assessment Dance—Step Two
Quick Qualifiers and Emotional Readiness

Once you've gotten the first encounter and Chemistry Connection Test over with, you can move on to more involved information gathering. Here are some things to look for as you date your Man Candidate the second, third, and even fourth times. Don't be shy about asking relevant questions, but you don't have to interrogate the guy either. Part of the process is learning if you enjoy spending time with someone and feel comfortable in his presence. On the other hand, give yourself a pep talk every time you go out with your candidate and set your mind on getting some answers. It's too easy to be afraid to be SMART and just go with the flow. Going with the flow too long is not what this book is about and is not SMART. You need to uncover the common ground and identify the no-go deal breakers to avoid Mr. Time Waster.

Man Hunt Interview Practices

As you spend time with your Man Candidate, consider that you are also interviewing him. Your aim is to discover as much relevant information about him as possible. Take it easy and don't rush things. Also, during the journey, remind yourself that perfect people do not exist so avoid the Perfectionism Ferris Wheel. Develop your interview strategy based on these suggested guidelines and remember, fun and smarts are success keys.

1. *Prepare to Tango*

Be prepared to share your thoughts and desires with Man Candidates when they ask for your viewpoint. You are entering a two-way street and should be ready to give your answer to the same questions that you ask him. This is a dance and is about getting to know each other, not about you putting him on trial. After all, it is only fair that if you ask him a tough question, you also have to answer a few. Guys like women with opinions and interests so be prepared to add value to the dance.

2. *Ask and Listen*

One of the most important approaches when interviewing Mr. Right is to use your active listening skills (see more information later in this chapter) when meeting with candidates. I cannot count the number of men and women who have said to me, "They were so into themselves and trying to prove that they were wonderful to me that I did not get in a word in the conversation."

There is nothing that turns someone off more than when you show that you are not listening to him or her by dominating the conversation. Your aim is to learn about your candidate, so ask your questions and let him do the majority of the talking. Use reflective statements such as, "You liked playing ice hockey in college. Tell me more about what you liked," to pull out his personality.

3. *Get the Facts First*

There are many ways to gather Foundational Facts about your Mr. Right candidates. You should work at uncovering this information within the first few communications and make mental notes as the facts unfold. Basic facts include age, height, weight, family structure, marital history/offspring, career, education, and hobbies.

If you use New Era options such as Internet dating or Professional Matchmakers, most of this data is already provided in a candidate's profile. In this case, you can skip the majority of this research step by quickly eliminating candidates that do not meet your basic requirements.

While, in many cases, guys will openly offer information about their family and friends, you can also start gathering facts using closed questions to make the process less intimidating. A closed question requires a one word or multiple-choice-type response. Using this technique, you can begin gathering Quick Qualifiers and Foundational Facts. For example, you can ask, "What are your favorite hobbies?" Another closed question might be, "How many siblings are in your family?"

4. Ask for Quick Qualifiers

Do you know your top three requirements in a mate? Can you describe your top three best attributes? Remind yourself to keep it light-hearted or you will scare the guy away. If this tango does not go well, it is no big deal, but it is simply time to exit the game early. The game is about getting to "Next" as soon as possible to avoid time wasters. Quick Qualifiers provide forward movement in the LIFE Match.

5. Discover the Real Man

Start using open questions to disclose more detail and look inside the man. You are trying to identify Mr. Right so begin building a comfort zone with a candidate to coax more honest responses to these open questions. For the best results, use LIFE Match Game Questions to discover the real man. (See more about this in Chapter Twelve.) Start slowly with some ice-breakers. For example, you might ask, "What was the happiest time of your life?" And then when you get more serious, you might ask, "Tell me why you have never been married before." Focus on areas that might help you discover Showstoppers. For example, if you are sure that you are not ready to be a step-mom, check out whether the man has children from a previous marriage early. Once you have uncovered a connection with a potential mate, you can start playing the LIFE Match Game more seriously.

6. Use the SMART ABC Man Codes

In order to provide you with some levity and practical solutions for identifying Mr. Right in the modern dating scene, Section IV contains the SMART ABC Man Codes. These valuable codes help you to assess what kind of man you have on your hands. Use the questions provided in the codes to confirm your initial assessment of your Man Candidate. Most men are a mixture of codes so you'll find your Man Candidate may be a number of them. And because you don't want to misinterpret someone, you might want to share the list of twenty-six A-Z codes with him and see which types he thinks apply. Make it a fun exercise and offer to share your codes as well. Since the questions are progressively more personal, use your judgment when trying them out. For example, on a second date try some of the Tell Me or ice-breaker questions listed first. In the end, you might not even need to ask your Man Candidate the answers, but can rely on active listening to learn what you need to know.

7. Mix it Up to Make it More Natural

Because a date is less structured than a job interview, feel free to mix up all of these interview practices. Don't go to every date with a formal agenda, give it time and let the information come out naturally. As long as you find major red flags early and avoid Mr. Time Waster, you want to give yourself some room for romance. Too much structure will damage the dance. While you can also make a lot of progress via email and phone discussions, avoid spending precious time on the LIFE Match

Game Questions at least until after the second live encounter. You do not need to know extreme detail about a Man Candidate until he passes the Chemistry Connection Test and Quick Qualifiers.

GATHER THE FOUNDATIONAL FACTS

If you meet a candidate through email introductions, international mixing, osmosis, or mutual friends, here are some fact-finding questions for your Mr. Right questionnaire. And again, take it easy because a lot of this information will be openly shared. Taking mental notes versus asking direct questions can be the easiest approach at this stage where you are just getting the facts.

Age, height, weight

How are old are you?
What age range are you interested in dating?
What is your height and weight?

Family Structure

How many siblings are in your family?
Where do you fall in the order of the siblings?
Are your parents still alive?
Do you have any nieces or nephews?

Marital History/Offspring

Have you ever been married?
Do you have any children?
If yes, what is the custody arrangement for the children?

Career

What have been your professional highlights?
Where did you go to school?
What are your future career goals?

Hobbies

What are your top three interests outside of work?
How many times a week do you like to exercise?
Are you interested in the arts?

Quick Qualifiers

With potential candidates, you can quickly determine the likelihood of a match by asking for the top three characteristics he desires in a soul mate. Be prepared to share three traits that best describe you and define your partner requirements list in return. These Quick Qualifiers are essential and can be gathered via email, phone, or in person with prospects. These facts will also help you quickly identify any relationship Showstoppers so you can immediately move to the next candidate.

As a single woman, being on the lookout for Quick Qualifiers helps me identify Man Candidates. For example, I attended a business networking event where I had qualifying discussions with two bachelors. Both men openly shared their thoughts so I was able to ask the men what they were looking for in a mate. As long as you keep the conversation light, you can find men who are happy to play this exchange game.

Bachelor # 1 wanted someone who can cook, is trustworthy and provides unconditional acceptance. Bachelor # 2 first responded, "It's all about chemistry." When I asked him to elaborate, he listed a sense of humor, adventurousness, and playfulness as his priorities in a mate.

I was instantly out of the game with Bachelor # 1 because I can barely boil water. Alternatively, my characteristics and needs more closely resembled Bachelor # 2's checklist. I look for someone who is worldly, passionate, and charismatic. I would also use these characteristics to describe myself. Not only did our top three needs harmonize, but there was also an immediate mutual attraction with Bachelor # 2. Because of these connections, we decided to have drinks the following week. I took a chance by asking these Quick Qualifying questions and ended up with a potential Man Candidate.

Recently, I polled people all over the country for their Quick Qualifiers. While there are some parallels, the answers show clear differences between the sexes and they are worth presenting here.

What Women Want

My single female friends value personality traits first. The top three things females are looking for are:

1. Good communication skills—ability to discuss, listen, and help problem solve

2. Sense of humor

3. Intelligence

In comparison, males listed sexual attraction as their top priority. Perhaps most women just assume sexual attraction as an obvious qualifier. However, the men were more obvious and blurted out this requirement.

What Men Want

The top three male preferences in female partners are:

1. Sex appeal—chemistry, looks

2. Sense of humor

3. Smarts—brains, intelligence

Overall, men and women have overlapping desires in a soul mate. So why is it so hard to find your special someone? Perhaps it is because people have different definitions of intelligence, sense of humor, and communication. What might be funny to you might not be funny to him. However, Quick Qualifiers will most likely help you identify connectors and roadblocks faster. Because time is precious, start using these Quick Qualifiers. If your top threes do not complement each other, it is time to say, Next.

Showstoppers

So what about the Showstoppers? Showstoppers are deal breakers. They may be in the form of different goals (a yes or no desire for children is a big one) or undesirable behavior (smoking is a common turn-off) but they stop all forward movement with a Man Candidate.

I had a win-win discussion with a Young Explorer (YE) who told me on our third date that while he used to think age was a Showstopper, he was more comfortable with older women and preferred their company over women his same age. While I had been initially nervous about the seven year gap in our ages, this discussion actually cleared up my anxiety about this potential Showstopper. What are your deal breakers?

Have you thought about your Showstoppers? In order to increase your awareness of what might break the deal, I took a daters poll and received this helpful list of what will make people walk. There are some clear similarities among the sexes and great insights in their comments.

SAMPLE SHOWSTOPPERS

She Said Showstoppers	He Said Showstoppers
"Caught Lying"	"Someone who is an actress."
"Bad manners is one of the most important parts of dating, no manners, no more dates."	"Lacks empathy"
"Extremely cheap"	"Too anxious to have marriage and kids"
"An arrogant man is a turn-off."	"Name droppers"
"Couch potato"	"No professional ambition"
"Rudeness to others"	"Overly talkative. And/or never reciprocates questions."
"Making last minute plans can be a red flag."	"Women who stress out and/or always talk/never listen."
"Obese"	"Poor grammar/writing in online situations."
"Lack of knowledge about basic etiquette"	"Charmless—her personality was boring"
"He should have a purpose or direction in life, not be wondering."	"Debt—I found out she was swimming in consumer debt."
"Excessive drinking, illegal drug use"	"Substance abuse of any kind: drugs, booze, cigarettes (can't stand 'em!)"
"Definitely smoking is a big red circle with a slash through it for me."	"Cigarette smokers are a definite turn-off."
"Unkept hair and lack of personal hygiene. His clothes should say that he thought to look nice for me."	"I wouldn't date someone who doesn't take care of herself—i.e., smokes, doesn't eat healthily, and doesn't exercise regularly"

QUICK QUALIFIERS AND SHOWSTOPPERS—TOP THREE

You can avoid wasting time with Man Candidates who have different agendas or conflicting requirements than you by using this worksheet as a guide. Don't take this sheet to your date, but throw out these questions in a light-hearted, almost "let's play a game" tone. You are in the early stages of dating so it's not time to get serious. Ask him for a list of his top three needs in a mate. Be willing to share your lists in return and remember to keep it fun versus placing the guy on trial.

A. What are the top three characteristics that are really important for you to find in Mrs. Right?

> 1.
>
> 2.
>
> 3.

B. Here are my top three characteristics that I use to describe Mr. Right:

> 1.
>
> 2.
>
> 3.

C. My top three best attributes include:

> 1.
>
> 2.
>
> 3.

(In case you are asked to describe yourself, prepare for this one and practice delivering it with a non-boastful tone.)

D. Are there any characteristics that are Showstoppers or deal breakers for either of you in a potential mate? Swap Showstoppers and give him some examples to spark the conversation.

1.

2.

3.

Emotional Readiness Test

An all important test at this stage of dating is Emotional Readiness and it's a real go/no go. Here's where you honestly ask yourself whether your Man Candidate is truly available. You're not just looking for clues as to whether he's involved with other women here, what you're looking for is whether this guy is *emotionally* ready for a real relationship. If he is not seeking a relationship, you are wasting your time and energy. A 32-year-old male entrepreneur also shared this perspective, he told me, "A guy will make himself available if he truly wants to be with a woman." So if he is not talking feelings or future with you within a reasonable start-up phase, maybe you are just not the right one for him and it's time for the Check Please!

The Emotional Readiness gauge can immediately make or break a long-term relationship deal. If you overlook the importance of Emotional Readiness, you might spend weeks, months and years fooling yourself with an unavailable candidate. There is a lot of truth to the statement, "Timing is everything."

Gauging Emotional Readiness is usually achieved by analyzing his responses to less direct questions. You probably want to tone down these statements on the first date. Avoid blurting out, "Are you ready to get married?" Using a direct question right off the bat may scare him, so watch for more subtle signs. For example, you might say, "I am tired of dating multiple people and really want to find a long-term relationship." If he responds with a similar viewpoint, then you know that you are in warm waters.

You can also approach Emotional Readiness lightly, by commenting with a big smile, "I promise that I won't ask you to marry me today, but I want you to know that I am trying to find a long-term partner." I tested this approach during Speed Dating and no one seemed to be taken aback by this comment. All the men I wanted to see again wanted to see me again as well, so this statement must not have scared them.

You can also try asking him:

- Do you like dating many people at one time or do you prefer monogamous relationships?

- Do think marriages can last today with the high divorce rate?

If he does not seem interested in responding to either of these statements, you are probably dealing with a player and you know what to do with these Sly Schemers: Just say, "Next."

Look for signs of Emotional Readiness as early as the second date. So long as you see *some* indication that it might be there, you can give him until the third date for further confirmation. If the potential partner does not seem interested in playing monogamous ball with you early in the game, it is time to find another opportunity. You are seriously seeking Mr. Right and cannot afford to waste precious time and energy on someone who is not emotionally ready. You want to be saying what my 40-something girlfriend told me about her husband-to-be, "There was no doubt in his mind that he wanted to be in a long-term committed relationship."

Signs of Emotional Readiness

Look for these signs when gauging the Emotional Readiness of a man:

- He is calling regularly to check in and ask about your day.

- He shows enthusiasm to see you by constantly setting up next dates.

- The guy shows a genuine interest in getting to know you and wants to hear your opinions.

- He becomes a cheerleader for your goals and interests.

- The guy makes you feel like a princess. He goes out of his way to bring you happiness and makes a habit out of saying and doing nice things.

- The guy tells you that he wants to take sex slow so you can build a bond first. (He is tired of playing the field and wants to get serious. I received a marriage proposal from this guy.)

- His actions match his words. He means what he says.

- And the biggest sign of Emotional Readiness is that he tells you that he wants a relationship and/or a future with you.

Pay Attention and Listen for the Answers

SMART Man Hunting is not only about asking the right questions at the right time, it is also about knowing when to just listen for the answers and pay attention to someone's behavior. Many times you don't even have to ask direct questions. The guy will hand you the answers and clues in conversation to help you make the right choices. While you can use the questions in this book directly, you can also find many answers in his statements and actions simply by raising your awareness.

Remember, you don't want to sound desperate or aggressive so this passive approach can be very effective and make the good GUT and red flag information come to you more naturally. I'm not saying don't ask questions. There are certain areas and times where you should probably be more direct (for example, when asking if someone is interested in a monogamous relationship.) However, you can gather a lot of information without ever having to ask by actively listening and being honest with yourself about what the signs are telling you.

Throughout the Man Hunt interview process, make mental notes and don't overlook the importance of casual conversation and actions. While someone may not have had a long-term relationship with you, their interactions with others can teach a lot about the person. Here are some examples of statements and signs revealed in casual conversation that can help you read between the lines.

ACTIVE LISTENING EXAMPLES

Casual Man Statements	Major Man Signs
"I watched the basketball game last night with my family. The game went into over-time and it was a blast."	This guy is a family man. He can have fun with his family, which is always a good sign for interpersonal relationships.
"The people at work drive me nuts because everyone has crazy ideas. I don't get why no one ever listens to my recommendations."	Watch out. This guy might not have the best interpersonal skills. He might have a tendency to blame others for his faults.
"I took my mother out to lunch today for Valentine's Day."	He is a potential keeper. He has a good relationship with his mother, which is always a good sign.

Casual Man Statements	Major Man Signs
"I have a bachelors' party weekend coming up. We are renting hotel rooms in Las Vegas. I don't know when I'll be back, but it should be a blast."	Warning—— Warning—Warning. This guy might be a Macho Mind, and we don't like guys who always place men first and treat women primarily as sex objects.
"When my father got really sick no one could tell us what was wrong so I kept calling friends until someone got me to the right doctor with the right diagnosis."	This guy is willing to stand by your side when the going gets tough. He is more likely to be there when you are old and gray so take a careful look at this man.
"I am having dinner tonight with friends and can see you afterwards for coffee."	This guy is not serious about you. He wants to keep you around but is not willing to share his life with you. Get out fast.

The Dating Assessment Dance—Step Two Wrap-Up

The second step in the Dating Assessment Dance is all about uncovering red flags and determining with whom you'd consider going to the mattresses. (You are literally determining not only who you might be inviting into the bedroom, but into the rest of your life.) Once you have completed your fact-finding mission, you should be able to make a go/no-go decision about your Man Candidate at this stage. No-go decisions will probably involve Showstoppers such as substance abuse or rudeness to others, or your belief that the Candidate is not Emotionally Available. Or maybe you've run across a Red Flag Man. However, if the Foundation is right, the Quick Qualifiers work and the GUT's good, use The LIFE Match Game Questions in the next chapter and continue to listen actively to help you take a closer look inside and identify your man.

CHAPTER TWELVE

The Dating Assessment Dance—Step Three
The LIFE Match Game

Have you knocked out all the Nos? Are you ready to go to the mattresses with the real players? By now you know that if there is no chemistry and the candidate is not Emotionally Ready (See more on the Bachelor Available in Section IV's "SMART Man Hunting ABC Man Codes"), you are wasting your time. The Quick Qualifiers and Showstoppers told you if there was a chance. By using closed questions to unveil Foundational Facts, you determined whether or not you want to dig deeper. You also eliminated the Red Flag Men and listened to your GUT about non-verbal warning signs.

Once you have identified a potential match who has passed all of your pre-tests, it's time to use LIFE Questions to look more deeply inside the man. You are now trying to identify Mr. Right candidates, and this can be the most challenging dance step. Remember that it is better to get this important information before you enter a life-long partnership. Gauge your Life Match Meter based on how your Man Candidate responds to these questions and then avoid blinders by taking time to observe his behavior. Is he a real deal?

Play the LIFE Match Game

If the candidate has made it this far, it's time to play the LIFE Match game. LIFE Match is about getting to know your Man Candidate on a deeper level in order to evaluate whether he could be a "life match" for you. By the third date, you should be comfortable enough to start asking these more revealing questions. LIFE Match revolves around gaining the following information:

L   Lessons Learned—What has he already learned in life?

I   Introspection—Can he be introspective and articulate his view on life and feelings?

F   Flexibility—Can he be flexible? Is he willing to compromise?

E   Extremes—What extremes exist in his life? Is he extreme about work or hobbies? Do you share his interests?

The LIFE Match Game is important for these reasons:

- It helps you further assess whether your Man Candidate is truly ready for or looking for a long-term commitment. If someone doesn't want to play LIFE Match, he's no match. I went out with a guy who told me on a third date, "Ask me any question you want. I am not afraid to answer anything." Remember, attitude is key, especially at this stage. If someone does not want to play, he is not real deal potential.

- You will learn what is important to your Man Candidate and how he views life. His answers to LIFE Match questions will enable you to determine the "fit" between you and your partner. LIFE Match will reveal glaring differences in life views as well as areas of agreement.

- LIFE Match reveals more than his answers. The most important part of the LIFE Match game is observing all the non-verbal clues your Man Candidate exhibits as he answers LIFE Match questions. As you play LIFE Match realize that the answers lie as much in his actions and in what he doesn't do as in what he says. If you want to be SMART, you'll look for this important information.

- Your analysis of LIFE Match willingness, questions, and non-verbal clues further helps you identify the SMART ABC Man Codes of your man. The ABC Man Coding keeps you from losing your head as you get to know your Man Candidate better. Realize that remaining clear and confidant ensures greater long-term success. You need to play the game with finesse, and that means maintaining a non-desperate vibe. So be ready to take-it-or-leave-it if things start going south. Don't try to force a match or the right answers. The purpose is to avoid the "D" word so why try to close a deal that has the wrong foundation or missing parts?

How do you play the LIFE Match Game?

1. Begin a Dance Dialogue

You are about to enter into an ongoing dance dialogue with a Mr. Right who could be a potential mate. This dialogue is a like a negotiation since you'll both be presenting your points of views and then deciding what you can and can't live with. Realize that, with this more personal level of exchange, you will begin building a solid foundation for a long-term relationship. If he is willing to play ball, start looking inside at the real man. Discuss your feelings, clarify your expectations, and ask him more about what he is feeling. Explain your personal goals. One 40-something girlfriend told me, "Tell him what you want in a non-threatening way and then see if he steps up to the plate."

2. Watch for Willingness on the Part of the Candidate

You are seeking a life partner, so anyone who does not want to start sharing on a deeper level at this stage is obviously not in the same ball-park. This third step is a fork in the road and requires some decisiveness on your part. You're either going to stick to your SMART Man Hunting guns by getting the information you need to fully evaluate someone or you risk wasting time on a Mr. Wrong. If the candidate is not willing to communicate and discuss life views, he is probably not sincerely interested in you as a person or in having a long-term commitment in his life. Decide whether he is working with you or exhibiting avoidance behavior when LIFE Questions come up. If you are not getting the results and respect that you desire at this point, take the nearest exit.

One 34-year-old Recruiter made this observation about her serious relationship with a 45-year-old writer. She said, "We both agree that a relationship is a vehicle for our own personal growth. Most men don't even understand what that sentence means." While you might not get this extreme buy-in from a man, look for the readiness clues.

If your Man Candidate is genuine and willing to engage in a LIFE Match dialogue, I recommend limiting LIFE Questions to in-person encounters. It's the non-verbal clues given during the dialogue that are critical during this stage so it's best to keep communication face-to-face.

3. Trust Your GUT

Based on his verbal and non-verbal responses, you will get a good sense of the person. Watch how he treats you and how he makes you feel inside to determine if he's got good GUT—is he Genuine, Understanding and Trustworthy?

Don't stop checking your basic GUT instincts, even after the Chemistry Connection Test. What are the dynamics between the two of you as the dating dance continues?

GUT Interaction Questions

Check your GUT regarding the way he works with you. You can use these GUT Interaction Questions to test your tango.

- Is there a good give-and-take exchange in this relationship?

- Does he actively listen to your concerns?

- Does he do what he says he will do?

- Does he treat you with kindness and consideration when you are together?

- Does he make your dates a priority or allow them to be interrupted by cell phone calls?

- Does he show good character when he interacts with people?

- Does he complement you both mentally and physically?

If you're going to grow old with Mr. Right, these interpersonal dynamics become even more critical. You want a life partner who can work with you and the way the two of you interact is an essential success factor. As my 45-year-old male CEO friend added, "Ask yourself whether you would want to get on a boat for a two-month sailing trip to Hawaii with the guy. Would you be better off as a couple in the end?" The reality test is about how the two of you work together as a team. The sexual passion will fade, and you need to be more concerned about what is going to last a lifetime.

Despite popular illusions of finding a perfect life, Ozzie and Harriett lives do not exist. Be SMART about selecting a man who will be there for the long haul.

4. Look Beyond Your GUT

Even if the GUT is good, it is still your job to uncover any potential major obstacles by asking the LIFE MATCH Questions. When my 30-something girlfriend was invited to move in with her boyfriend, she told me, "I need to ask him some of your LIFE questions first. We need to have more conversations before I move into his house. I'm not sure if we share the same long-term goals of marriage and children." A man can have great GUT but may still see or want things differently from you. In fact, you should be even more careful when there's GUT because this candidate may truly be the "one." But you won't find out if you don't continue to play LIFE Match.

5. Accept That There Are No Right or Wrong Answers

There are no right or wrong answers to LIFE Questions so it's not fair judging anyone on what they have to say. Remember you're just looking for a match. The right answer depends on your needs and desires. How do you mesh with this candidate's views? Does his way of life complement your lifestyle? Can he be flexible? These are the questions for you to ask during this interview phase. And don't forget the GUT factor.

6. Round One: First Look Inside

You can start with icebreaker questions to ease into the game. Discover how someone has handled the ups and downs on his life's journey. Find out more about his viewpoints by using this "Tell Me" method. Because you cannot predict the future, Tell Me Questions illuminate how the Candidate has handled various situations in the past and whether he is able to learn from his mistakes. Use these LIFE Match Game Round One questions to start your review of the Total Man. You can even make a game out of this exchange. Offer to share your answers if he agrees to enter this tango with you. And don't forget to listen for the answers along the journey. He will probably tell you the answers to some of these questions without you even asking.

Round One Tell Me Questions

- Tell me what activities you like to share with your mate.

- Tell me how often you attend sports games and who usually goes with you.

- Tell me about your happiest moment and what happened.

- Tell me about your scariest time and what happened.

- Tell me about your greatest personal achievement and why it was so important to you.

- Tell me about the most exciting time of your career.

- Tell me about the most challenging time of your career.

- Tell me about what you think makes a great friendship.

- Tell me about someone whom you were able to help with a problem.

- Tell me about what you think makes a great marriage.

7. *Round 2: ABC Man Code Analysis*

While gathering information with Round One Tell Me Questions, you will start to learn more about the ABCs of your Man Candidates. In Section IV, you'll find the SMART ABC Man Codes that apply to your Man. These codes provide more food for thought and shed light on situations using real-life scenarios as examples. You may want to go back to Round One and ask more questions before proceeding to your Final Man Analysis. You will also find the ABC Man Codes help you develop success strategies for working well with your Man Candidate.

After months of dating the wrong men in Los Angeles, I created these Man Codes as a way to bring levity to my search for Mr. Right. These male dating codes are not based on science and are intended to provide you with some reality checks by asking you to think more clearly about a Man Candidate. In these descriptions, you will find a balanced array of personalities that include both desirable and undesirable guys. You might find that your personality also fits one of the codes. Many of the ABC codes are not gender specific even though the examples in this code book are all male. Interestingly, many men have asked, "Tell me what is your code?" It's easy to apply these codes to women. For example, a BA can be a Bachelor Available or a Bachelorette Available—so be prepared to join in the fun and share your codes with a man.

The definitions, true-story examples, and strategies in the codes are designed to help you quickly determine whether a candidate meets your needs. What works for you might not be a match for somebody else. You might find a Man candidate represents several of these ABC man acronyms. Use the LIFE Questions recommended in the codes to disclose his patterns and priorities. The goal is to find a male with a code(s) that complements your personality while avoiding the rotten eggs or elephant in the room.

Use these SMART ABC Man Codes to gather additional insights and make even better Mr. Right decisions. Extremes are especially important. As one 30-something woman commented about the code book, "It's hard for some people to clear out the cobwebs and impressions get clouded. The codes help you tune in to your radar." Even though someone expresses an interest in a hobby or is career-oriented, you will not know the extreme until you ask for more information. You also need to take time to get to know the person to see if his behavior corresponds with his answers. One Man Candidate went so far as to ask a woman I know to marry him. An avid sailor, he neglected to consider or reveal his long range plan of devoting the rest of his life to his hobby. He saw nothing wrong in leaving his partner behind for weeks or months at a time "holding down the fort."

8. *Gauge Your Life Match Meters*

At this point in the game, it is time to check the gauge on your LIFE Match Meter with Mr. Right candidates. It's time to decide how long you want to play the game with a particular candidate. If you are not sure about a man, one 40-year-old girlfriend told me, "Write a Pro and Con list." You are not going to find Mr. Perfect because he doesn't exist, but you may find Mr. Perfect Match. Decide whether the Pros outweigh the Cons.

Give your potential match a rating on a scale of 1-10. If he receives at least a 9, then you may have found a life mate. Guys have been rating women from 1–10 for years on the front steps of fraternity houses and inside locker rooms so why shouldn't we do it? Only this time, the rating is much more important. We now have SMART strategies to help us make good choices versus simply reacting to a guy's appearance walking down the street. Similar to the corporate world where 95% is a typical goal for quality, you need to set high standards and mine for the gold. Anything below a 9 is not okay with me.

Start gauging the results of your LIFE Match Game. Do you want the same things? Do you have the same values? Does he want to make it work with you? Can you live with his approach to life?

LIFE MATCH METERS

A. What are Mr. Right's ABC Codes? What are your Codes?

B. What LIFE Questions do I still need to ask?

C. What are the Pros and Cons of this Man Candidate?

Man Pros: Man Cons:

D. What is your Life Match Meter rating for this Man?

Circle your overall LIFE Match Meter rating for this Man Candidate:

1   2   3   4   5   6   7   8   9   10

If your gauge is heavily leaning towards a Match, but you still need more information, go back to Round One. If your Gauge and your GUT tell you that this could be the "one," proceed to step 9, below. If he did not receive at least a 9 on the LIFE Match Meter, he is not your man. It's time to go back to SMART Man Hunting.

9. *Review the Total Man—Final ABC Man Analysis*

The Life Match Gauge helps you to review the total man, but the Final Man Analysis uses the SMART ABC Man Codes to put everything into perspective for you. Many teachers will tell you that the best way to learn is by example. These Man Codes and examples were based on a balance of good and bad male encounters. Use the codes to save yourself weeks, months and even years with Mr. Wrong. The most important part about the Final Man Analysis is not just deciding when you have a Mr. Right on your hands, but being honest with yourself when someone is a Mr. Wrong. The sooner you make this decision the better.

MR. WRONG CASE STUDIES

In order to help you avoid prolonged heartache and know when to walk, here are three Mr. Wrong Case Studies. Each case illustrates a very common mistake women make in the dating game. If you make this mistake don't sweat it. And don't let it stop you from being proactive. Remember, there are a lot of men out there and every dating dance gets you a little closer towards identifying a Mr. Right. You are getting SMARTer every day.

Mr. Wrong # 1—The Elephant in the Room

Watch out for the Elephant in the Room or the man with the hidden undesirable code. Check out this combination and tale.

ABC Codes:

- Bachelor Available (BA)

- Curious Male/Female (CMF)

- Keeper of the Fire (KOF)

- Social Guru (SG)

- Questionnaire Perfectionist (QP) (the elephant)

Sometimes what makes the Final Man Analysis so tricky is that a Candidate will fall into one or more good code categories while also exhibiting one or two undesirable code categories. It's too easy to overlook the latter because you're so happy to have found the former. Remember all these codes are usually always present from the get-go. It's about being honest enough with yourself to admit that they are there. For example, this Mr. Wrong came off as everything a woman could want. He was available (BA), comfortable in his masculinity and open to female friendship (CMF), devoted (KOF), and social (SG). This example illustrates what happens when one trait that doesn't work for you can negate all the other positive traits. Don't ignore the elephant in the room or you'll regret it later.

This dreamboat had his honey on cloud nine for years, even down the wedding path. But soon after marriage, the bride in this case was forced out of the clouds when her mate's personality extremes and his QP (Questionnaire Perfectionist) tendencies destroyed the relationship. This man was unwilling to compromise from his requirements checklist. For example, he wanted his wife to cook dinner at home every night during the week to save money and spend quality time together. When she offered to compromise by sharing dinner three times a week, this solution was not good enough for him. Ultimately, this demanding perfectionist's expectations affected all areas of the marriage and became the elephant in the room.

Mr. Wrong # 1 Moral: Look for all the codes and never deny the existence of the less attractive ones. They're always the most important and will grow to elephantine proportions eventually.

Mr. Wrong # 2 The Too Perfect Transformer

What about the guy who changes his tune? He might have great codes, but give it some time and he might just blind-side you with a new attitude.

ABC Codes:

- Bachelor Available (BA)

- Curious Male/Female (CMF)

- Keeper of the Fire (KOF)

- Nourishing Nester (NN)

- Hello Good-bye Guy (HGG) (What happened?)

You know those children's toys that look like action heroes but with the flip of a few parts transform into gross insects? That's what this guy is. This Too Perfect Performer is an example of someone who seems to be a real Mr. Click. He has all the right codes and the actions to back them up. While dreams do come true, beware of the men who are too perfect. Mr. Click took his date to a great French restaurant on the first date, brought her one of his favorite CDs on the second date, and arrived with flowers on the third date. He called every day to hear about her day and indicated that he had a strong interest in a relationship. After three dates with Mr. Click, he showed all the promising signs of the SMART ABC Man Codes above.

However, three weeks into intense dating with Mr. Click, he suddenly turned into an HGG (Hello Goodbye Guy.) Without any explanation other than a busy work schedule, he suddenly dropped off the face of the earth, leaving his date to wonder why. It may have been because she refused to sleep with him on the third date, which actually makes him a Sly Schemer (see Red Flag Men in Chapter Ten.) On the other hand, anything can send a HGG scurrying for the hills. The point is you'll never know why he changed his tune.

Mr. Wrong # 2 Moral: Always take the time to allow a man to reveal his true colors or codes. A wise 32-year-old girlfriend who is happily married said to me, "You need to give it time. Ask questions and then observe to see if they do what they say, and avoid salespeople." She added, "Ask yourself, does he walk the talk?"

While you do the dance, don't put your eggs all in one basket and keep dating, even if he is a Mr. Click. And when a Mr. Click turns into a transformer, don't let this mind-boggling unexpected twist get you down. And don't give yourself a hard time because your intuition was wrong—simply move forward. Better to find out sooner rather than later that Mr. Click turned out to be Mr. Wrong.

Mr. Wrong # 3 Missing Ingredient

Beware of men who seem great, but are missing key ingredients. Don't forget to wear your glasses when making a Final Man Analysis.

ABC Codes:

- Curious Male/Female (CMF)

- Nourishing Nester (NN)

- Post Traumatic Soul (PTS)

Sometimes a key code will be missing in a Man Candidate and for some reason you don't notice. Usually you're blinded by what's going on in your own life or due to neediness. When a Man Candidate's other codes fill a need in us, we'll miss a salient point, like whether he is Emotionally Ready.

Take, for example, the story of a 37-year-old business executive who met a same-aged TV Producer during the week of the Northridge earthquake in Los Angeles. A long distance relationship ensued for months afterwards. The couple spent hours on the phone talking about the 6.7 earthquake and helping each other through the recovery period. So what happened? She wasn't paying attention to her code book. She wasn't asking the right LIFE Questions. That's because this guy was filling an important need for her. Both people were experiencing a case of post traumatic stress disorder and needed an intimate friend at that time. This type of connection happens quite frequently. After months of conversations, the woman finally admitted what was there all along: That the TV Producer was not a BA (Bachelor Available.) Yes, he liked her, but he had no intention of walking down the aisle with her.

Mr. Wrong # 3 Moral: Be aware when you're having some issues or unmet needs because that's when this type of Mr. Wrong is going to walk into your life. You can deal with your needs on your own or you can date this Mr. Wrong. There's nothing wrong with this comfort man. Just be clear about what is happening and don't talk yourself into thinking a guy who happens to be there when you need him is a Mr. Right. Be grateful for what you received and move on without regrets. You've probably made a pretty good friend.

Who is Mr. Perfect?

We all have an image of what we think we want consciously. However, as my 45-year-old male CEO friend clarified to me, "The reality is that we are often ruled by the subconscious that is driven by the heart." We have all been influenced by the media to create a Mr. Perfect image in our minds, but our reality man may be something very different.

In the final analysis, sometimes your Mr. Perfect has to give in to GUT considerations. In the three examples of Mr. Wrong described previously, each woman was misled by her belief that the man in question matched her idea of Mr. Perfect. In the end those Mr. Wrongs did not have the crucial combination of GUT and LIFE Match. This misread serves to illustrate the importance of GUT over Mr. Perfect as well as how important it is to continue to play the LIFE Match Game throughout your dating journey with a Man Candidate so you can continually check on his GUT—and yours.

Who is Mr. Perfect to you? What real life traits or actions do you look for in your search for Mr. Right? Here's what some daters have to say about what tells them they've found Mr. or Ms. Right.

THE RIGHT STUFF

She Observes Mr. Right Material	He Observes Mrs. Right Material
"Little things like small touches, cooking, going to places, events, outings he really isn't interested in just because you are there."	"Listening is big with me. Someone who will listen attentively. "
"Consideration, in everyday parts of life, whether it is holding the door, cooking dinner, or other."	"Do they present themselves well? Are they stylish. . .but not overly so? Are they attractive but not flamboyant?"
"Other stuff, a good dancer, good taste in general, clothes, music, manners, does he believe men open doors?"	"A sparkle in her eyes and softening of her facial features when I enter the room."

She Observes Mr. Right Material	He Observes Mrs. Right Material
"He watches you (you see him, but he doesn't know you've caught him) doing mundane tasks."	"I look for smiles—people who smile a lot are usually happy people—I like happy people."
"Either sits too close or too far away. (I want them to have a sense of space.)"	"It's manners. Eye contact, touching, listening, enthusiasm, and the way she carries herself."
"Must be confident enough to maintain eye contact when talking to you."	"How they interact in social settings. Do they mingle? Are they comfortable talking with strangers? Do they listen?"
"He is focused on 'us' and not scanning the crowd for something better. He appears confident and at ease."	"Someone that makes my heart race when the phone rings and it could be her. Someone who I look forward to seeing more every time we spend together."
"Mr. Right must be sensitive and touch me once in a while when speaking."	"It's the way she likes you even when you're wrong."
"Being a nice guy in traffic. Showing restraint when matters get tough, at the airport, or when someone is really being slow behind a counter somewhere."	"It's a turn of the wrist or flip of the hair, a timbre in her voice, a sparkling in her eyes."

Mr. Perfect Only Happens in the Movies

Let's go to the movies for a good example of a fantasy romance. Only Hollywood can produce this kind of Mr. Perfect. He doesn't exist in real life. But this Mr. Right does pass all the SMART Man Hunting tests, so let's have a look at him anyway. The characters played by Meg Ryan and Hugh Jackman in the movie *Kate and Leopold* share a passionate Chemistry Connection immediately. Not only that, there are many signs of an excellent match. You can see that he clearly passes the Emotional Readiness Test when, in their first few scenes together, the eye contact is powerful and he expresses a strong desire to get married. You can also look at his ABC Man Codes to explain why Leopold is a dream match.

Mr. Fantasy Codes:

- Bachelor Available (BA) He expresses a desire to get married, but to the right one. He shows a genuine interest in finding a soul mate.

- Keeper of the Fire (KOF) Leopold is a pro in the romance department. He makes her toast with butter and strawberries for breakfast. He sends her romantic letters. When she leaves for work, he helps Kate put on her coat. These are only a few of the countless KOF examples in the movie.

- Nourishing Nester (NN) He cooks her gourmet dinners and carries Kate to bed when she is tired. He is sincerely concerned for her welfare.

So what about the GUT feeling Kate has for Leopold? When she presents him as an actor candidate for a butter commercial, she tells her boss, "He's a dream. He's handsome, honest, courteous, and stands up when you walk in the room." Leopold's advice to Kate's brother also shows signs of good character. While the brother prepares to call a woman for a date, Leopold tells him, "Women respond to sincerity."

This is a Mr. Perfect indeed. Trouble is you're only going to find him in the movies. Clearly, movie producers, writers and directors know what women are looking for and can create fantasies for them on the big screen.

Check the Core GUT for a Perfect Match

So how do you recognize a Mr. Right? Let's take a look at a Real-Life Perfect Match with all the right ingredients for long-term success.

The Perfect Tango

Remember the story about my piano teacher who met her life partner taking tango dance lessons in the "Jump into Your Passions" section in Chapter Four? She was engaged in ten days, living with him after three months, pregnant at seven months and married on the date of their son's birth. This couple represents the Perfect Tango. Based on the dynamics of their dance, you can understand why she rates her Mr. Perfect Match as a ten on the LIFE Match Meter.

When the couple met three years ago, she was a 34-year-old pianist and he was a 46-year-old entrepreneur. Both partners exuded great confidence and a sense of self. They were experienced daters, which made it easier for them to identify their soul mate.

Both parties passed the Chemistry Connection Test and Emotional Readiness Test on the first date. After ten days, they were engaged. How did the couple know so fast that they had found their soul mates? When I asked her to describe why she knew, her first response was tied to a

GUT reaction: "I knew that he was honest with good intentions, and not pretentious." She continued by adding, "He didn't talk about himself. He was very interested in my ideas and was a patient and attentive listener."

If you ask him to explain it, he says, "I was good at developing radar for a good match after being on the dating circuit for five years and after having married twice for the wrong reasons. I knew pretty quickly that she had all the ingredients. After ten days of dating, I knew that I had found my life partner."

When I asked whether she used any LIFE Questions to review his character and go beyond the GUT, she explained this observation, "Well he had a great relationship with his mother that was really balanced and strong. He treats his mother with great respect, and that was very appealing to me." The couple also shares the same sense of humor and a similar interest in marketing. He added, "We were so compatible. I could finish her sentences and she could finish mine." She added, "We shared the same morals and value systems."

So what type of SMART ABC Man Codes does she use to describe her perfect match?

Mr. Perfect Match

- Bachelor Available (BA) He was definitely emotionally available for a lasting relationship. After five years of dating, he was ready to settle down with a mate.

- Nourishing Nester (NN) He genuinely cares about her best interest and enjoys spending time with her at home. He said to me, "I don't need to be at parties and events. Being with her is enough for me."

- Keeper of the Fire (KOF) She thinks he is very romantic at heart. He told me, "I continually try to maintain and earn respect from her. I like to hold doors for her, help her with the groceries, and never ignore her at a party even if there are good looking women there."

- Curious Male/Female (CMF) She told me, "He is very nice to other women and has female friends." He sets boundaries with his female contacts, and the interactions make him a more balanced male.

- Guy with Offspring (GWO) Mr. Perfect Match had two seven-year-old twin girls from a previous marriage when they met. When I asked her how she felt about the kids, she commented, "I wasn't concerned because I loved him so much. I would be more concerned if he was a 46-year-old that had never been married."

What has made their relationship remain so strong after a wedding and baby boy? First, she commented, "There is a mutual respect for each other. He is one hundred percent behind me and I completely back him. If you are both striving to make your partner look good, you can't go wrong." In addition, the couple highlights their flexible approach to life as a key to their success. In reference to give-and-take, he noted, "It is natural between us. There is no scorecard. There is no manipulation or lying in our relationship, and it feels great."

While it may be hard to believe, she explained, "We've never had an argument or a fight." He added, "Sometimes we joke yell at each other and pull pranks, but we know it is not serious because we just don't fight."

In reference to previous partners, he told me, "I don't have problems with ex-boyfriends as long as they were nice to her. I'm not the jealous type, but there are many out there who are that way."

She explained their marriage dynamics further to me: "We would do anything for each other, but would never take advantage of one another. There are just too many selfish people out there, and so many relationships get destroyed by an accounting approach of continually keeping track of who did what for the other."

In the end, the happy husband summarized this Perfect Match by stating, "I'm so satisfied with her that I would never be tempted by another. She is really my number one priority in life and maintaining our relationship is a continual process." Her final statement to me was "I don't want our story to seem like a fantasy. We're not perfect people and we don't have perfect lives. We deal with life issues every day, but I'm glad that I'm in the game with him." Based on the Final Man Analysis, this relationship is clearly built to last.

The Perfect Match Exists

While there is no such thing as a Perfect Person, there is a Perfect Match out there for you. Look for good GUT and always check LIFE Match. It might also be time to let go of your ideas about Mr. Perfect. Sometimes our fantasies keep us from the Perfect Match since we eliminate perfectly good Mr. Rights over missing Mr. Perfect qualities. As a 50-year-old female CEO put it: "We can rationalize our way out of anything as an adult and never make a decision." At a certain point, you will need to decide if you are willing to take a chance to go the distance.

Be Proactive

If you want the Perfect Match you have to be proactive. One of my closest girlfriends set a goal on her 40th birthday to be married or engaged by the end of that year. She bumped into someone special through osmosis during the same month. She actually had met her Mr. Right ten years earlier at a wedding. My 40-year-old girlfriend had great success with this man because she used SMART Man Hunting techniques to evaluate her Mr. Right. She made her goals very clear out of the gate, kept an open dialogue, no bull policy, and found herself engaged by the end of the year to a genuine and considerate 44-year-old real-estate professional. His comment to me at their engagement party was, "I think she is wonderful. Even though we have differences, I don't even think about changing her. I love her for the way she is, and that is all that matters."

Another 35-year-old Financial Manager, whom I coached, set a goal to date ten men between April and December one year. Simply by stepping out and actively dating, she boosted her ego, met more high-quality men, and ended up walking down the aisle two years later with one of the guys she met on her Man Hunt journey.

The Test of Time

Why are GUT and LIFE Match so important? Take a look at my parents' forty year marriage. My mother always told me that she had a really good GUT feeling when she met my father on a blind date.

When you ask my parents how they lasted so long, my mother will respond, "The only thing that is certain in life is change so it is all about how you handle the turns in life together." Because my parents are both flexible and have compromised over the years, they have created a lasting give-and-take relationship. They have been able to weave their way successfully through the partnership journey. And as my father told me,

"It's all about your attitude towards life. When you think you've got it made, it all goes bad. When you think it can't get worse, it always gets better. It is important to find someone whom you love and can roll with the punches. Your mother and I love each other and have fun together. We adjust in life."

In the end, it is the dynamics of the dance that makes a relationship go the distance. Dating assessment is a dance too, one that reveals how our partner will do the dance of Lifetime partnership. If the dance isn't going well in the dating phase, it won't work in marriage either. That's why the Dating Assessment Dance is the way to go to be SMART.

You Go Girl!

If you learn by example, take chances, smile, ask the right questions, pay attention, present a positive persona, and know when to quit, you will have a successful Man Hunt journey. Use your new SMART dating skills on top of what you already know to achieve better results.

The New Era Dating Options provide women with endless possibilities for finding the right life partner. Expand your bandwidth, wear confidence, and start searching smarter and safely because you are now SMART Man Hunting Certified for success! And if, in the end, you meet Mr. Right through osmosis, with all the practice you're going to have from SMART Man Hunting, you'll know how to find out if he's a Mr. Right or even a Perfect Match. In the meantime, more power to you for getting out there, taking chances, bouncing back from rejection, boosting your ego, and for bravely taking the Mr. Right search road. You might just look back in five years and say to yourself, "Wow, that was a great journey."

And if people tell you that men don't want to get married anymore, do not believe what you hear. Here is an insight from a 29-year-old consultant who is engaged to a 32-year-old woman. He shared a secret with me: "People say guys are terrified of getting married. I think they're only scared if it's the wrong person." Well, you be too. Follow the SMART Man Hunting plan for success and you'll ensure a more viable relationship in the long term.

With these new insights, SMART ABC Man Codes and Interview Practices, you are ready to meet the challenge of proactively searching for Mr. Right. You were already smart, but now you are SMARTer:

S   Search proactively for Mr. Right with confidence, using New Era dating options

M   Meet more high-quality men and boost your ego, while following SMART safety guidelines

A   Assess candidates to identify real deal LIFE potential in the Dating Assessment Dance

R   Review the Total Man, using the SMART ABC Man Codes and Final Man Analysis

T   Trust your GUT instincts and LIFE Match results to find your Perfect Match

SECTION IV

The SMART Man Hunting ABC Man Codes

SMART ABC Man Codes Definitions, Tales, and Strategies

Are you ready to learn from the successes and failures of other dating experts? Use these SMART ABC Man Codes, definitions, examples, and strategies to identify patterns, encourage healthy dialogue and have some fun along your dating journey. You don't want to overlook important characteristic complements and clashes when identifying Mr. Right so let this code book be your compatibility guide.

Because dating can be a struggle, you can also use some comic relief along the way so have some laughs with the code names. Hopefully, you can also laugh at your mistakes by using these dating story reminders. We have all made mistakes so don't be hard on yourself. Instead, give yourself a break. Applaud yourself for getting smarter with every relationship and allow room for laughter. It's the best survival strategy for dating.

What are these SMART ABC Man Codes? How can they help you with your Man Hunt? This code book will help you identify Man Candidate characteristics and to create a dating success strategy. You now have Man Candidates. Are you ready to take a closer look inside to determine whether your needs match his priorities, style and desires? The SMART ABC Man Codes in this Section provide both humor and reality checks to ensure dating success. Similar to the acronym soup used to reference corporate departments and organizations, these ABC abbreviations provide women with their own glossary to New Era men and serve as a reference for the Dating Assessment Dance. Each code is an acronym for a type of Man Candidate. It is supported by a code definition, a Man example, and recommended strategies and questions for this type of Man.

These Man Codes are based on the experience of female dating insiders and will save you time and energy in your Man Hunt. By recognizing the types of Man Candidates out there, it helps you cut-to-the-chase in your Dating Assessments and Man Interview Practices by helping you gain clarity on the Mr. Wrongs as well as the Mr. Rights. Refer to the dating strategy guidelines to avoid lengthy dating disasters that damage your ego and steal you away from checking out other opportunities. This SMART ABC Man Code Book can help you find your soul mate faster with a much greater ROI (Return on Investment.)

The Man Codes do not have to be read in A-Z order. If the code for a potential mate jumps right out at you, feel free to go directly to that description and its recommended strategies. You can even share this reference guide with a potential match. Ask him to identify his codes and then see how your perceptions compare. I shared these New Era Man Codes with one potential candidate and compared notes. While I thought he was an OO (Over-Achiever Obsessor), he defined himself as a KOF (Keeper of the Fire) and PTS (Post Traumatic Soul). Because of a tough loss of a loved one, he was just not ready to be a BA (Bachelor Available). I learned a lot about him from this discussion and we grew closer as a result.

And don't forget, even though the examples are all male, the codes can apply to women as well. Take an honest look at your own priorities and preferences when reviewing these male types. What are your woman codes? How do they mesh with your man's codes? For example, if you are a NN (Nourishing Nester) who prefers quiet time at home, you might clash with a male SG (Social Guru) who thrives in a crowd.

Use the ABC Man Codes to gauge your Man Candidate on the LIFE Match Meter and as you do the Dating Assessment Dance. Use the LIFE Questions in the Codes or formulate your own to identify what codes belong to you current Man Candidates. You want to uncover similar goals and then address anything that does not sit well now versus later if you are headed down the wedding-bell path.

Selecting a Mr. Right is not easy. It's a delicate two-way dance. In addition to the LIFE Questions, the dating strategies will give you another way to observe his behavior and listen for the red flags. Remember to use the Winning Hunter's Toolkit by packing your life skills set of confidence, patience and persistence versus giving off desperate or needy vibes to lead you to success at this juncture. Even though you are further along the dating journey, you can still gather vital information without being too serious.

Are you ready to have some fun in the final phase of your man hunt journey? By placing these codes and dating strategies in your purse, you will not only have some comic relief, but be able to make smarter Man choices. Have fun with the codes. They can only make you SMARTer and increase your odds of identifying Mr. Right, and that's what this journey is all about.

ASF—All Sports Fanatic

All Sports Fanatic Definition

The All Sports Fanatic (ASF) can be the a woman's worst nightmare because his obsession has been developed over decades and may even be hereditary. The ASF is completely consumed with following his sports heroes, tends to be a season ticket holder, and usually lives and dies by the won-lost log and box scores.

Every weekend, ASFs are either at the game or in front of the television. His conversations mostly concern upcoming sports events, game results, and player statistics. He has a sport for every season and constantly looks for opportunities to discuss this fixation.

All Sports Fanatic Example

Recently, a girlfriend in her 30s married a 38-year-old ASF. Although he has had a successful Financial Accounting career, his real passion is following football and basketball.

She knew from the beginning that he was an ASF. All weekend activities revolved around meeting his buddies to watch the games. Sometimes the girlfriends and wives were included, but mostly they were all-male rallies. While she also enjoyed watching sports, my friend had interests as well in movies and cultural activities. As a result, she was able to find a balance by giving him room to go off with his fellow fanatics.

When they got engaged in February, I asked her if we could go to dinner to celebrate. She responded by saying, "After college basketball season in early April." An even bigger surprise was that she didn't seem to mind the wait to accommodate her fiancé's tunnel vision. Apparently, that was just the way the ball bounced.

Later, I learned more about the seriousness of this obsession when my boyfriend and I joined the couple at University of Maryland basketball games. The ASF got so consumed with his team's performance that if they were behind it would ruin his entire evening. He would be silent throughout the game and depressed for several days if they lost. This ASF also placed basketball bets in Las Vegas over the Internet. Overall, he takes the game a little too seriously for me.

The couple is still happily married. Not only has my friend accepted her mate's lifestyle; she has become great friends with his buddies' wives and maintained her own interests. More power to her and to you—that is, if you don't mind jumping through hoops for your ASF.

All Sports Fanatic Strategies

ASFs are as loyal to their sports teams as if they have given birth to them. Don't fool yourself that once you are married, things might change. If you have zero interest in sports, the ASF is so extreme in his fandom that you probably should not consider this candidate as a long-term partner unless you don't mind sitting on the bench a lot. On the other hand, if you are a cheerleader for the same teams, you could be ideal for one another.

The best way for you to be successful dating or marrying an ASF is to accept his lifestyle and build your own interests. If you find yourself entering a relationship with an ASF, test the waters by seeking compromise with some shared activities. For example, ask him if he is willing to go to the theater with you occasionally. You do not need to do everything together. However, you should establish a give-and-take relationship with compromise so that it is a win-win situation.

In addition, consider giving him a separate room for his hall-of-fame autographed pictures or you may find yourself living in a replica of Cal Ripken's locker. This sports memorabilia may dominate your walls. An extra bedroom or den might be a great way to contain the sports paraphernalia your guy lives to collect.

Because ASFs may have many redeeming qualities, they can be excellent partners despite this addiction. Don't allow this one element to halt a relationship but do consider the full package.

All Sports Fanatic LIFE Questions

1. Tell me about the sports teams that you follow.

2. Tell me how many times a week you like to watch games.

3. Tell me about your favorite sports hero and why.

BA—Bachelor Available

Bachelor Available Definition

A Bachelor Available (BA) is someone who is mentally and emotionally ready for a long-term commitment. These men are not always easy to find, but once a connection is established BAs openly tell you their intentions. You often find BAs using Internet dating or Professional Matchmakers because most men will not try these options until they are serious about finding a soul mate. BAs usually have the best intentions in mind and will value you as an individual.

Bachelor Available Examples

I have two examples of BAs to support the notion that willing and able prospects exist.

The first BA candidate was someone I met through an Internet dating introduction. We shared similar interests in horses, photography and travel. He showed genuine interest and concern for my needs, an approach that was a refreshing change from some of the other men I had encountered.

Dates with this BA were unique and romantic. He showed great effort to organize fun activities that interested both of us. For example, he took me to a private museum tour on a Tuesday during lunch. Because he desired a long-term relationship with me, this BA was also willing to move at a pace that was comfortable for me physically.

The second BA candidate was more blatant about his intentions. He had been primarily a friend, who later started asking me out. After two dates, he told me at lunch in a busy restaurant, "I am ready for a commitment so you just let me know when you are ready." I was so blown

B away as well as uncertain about my feelings for him that I did not know how to respond. Eventually, I realized that his romantic feelings were not mutual, and have fortunately been able to maintain a valuable friendship with this BA.

Bachelor Available Strategies

If you feel a mutual mental and physical connection with a BA, he is an ideal mate.

You should only consider serious relationships with BAs. If a prospect is not Emotionally Ready, you are wasting your time even if there are other code connections with him.

However, strategies with BAs will vary depending on your connection with the candidate. Even though you may not be as certain about the match right out of the gate as the BA, if there is any potential, don't walk away immediately. Because it can take time to fully appreciate someone, you may learn to adore this individual. Now that you are looking for a lifetime mate, other things become more important than just a physical attraction, and BAs are hard to find.

On the other hand, if you are confident there is no future with your BA, be delicately honest right away. BAs can be more vulnerable because they generally make their intentions clear up-front. If you drag things out, it is like a slow torture for these often sensitive men. Let them go so the BA can move forward with someone else that shares a mutual connection.

Bachelor Available LIFE Questions

1. Tell me about the type of relationship that you are looking to find.

2. What do you think makes a really good marriage?

3. Tell me about your long-term goals for a relationship.

CMF—Curious Male/Female

Curious Male/Female Definition

The Curious Male/Female (CMF) is another great catch because of his balanced personality. These males are confident and comfortable with their own masculinity—yet also enjoy the company and interests of women. CMFs often grew up with strong bonds to sisters and mothers, and, as a result, value female relationships. Such men will choose dinner with you or other couples over a guys' night out. CMFs will go to the movies or theater with you, but will also have male friendships. Because CMFs represent balance, they can be ideal mates.

Curious Male/Female Example

My 35-year-old girlfriend dated a classic example of a Curious Male/Female. He is an athletic 39-year-old CEO of two businesses. While this CMF shares his passion for extreme sports with male friends, he is equally enthusiastic about calling female friends to go roller-blading. He grew up with a brother and sister and had a devoted relationship to his mother. During my friend's relationship with him, this CMF was comfortable discussing his feelings and regularly compromised on activities so both of their needs were met.

For example, on a typical Saturday, this CMF might go to the spa with my girlfriend, and then later ride horses at the track with his buddies. He also organized group dinners and activities with both male and female friends. An example of this CMF's natural curiosity about women is that he offered to attend the *Vagina Monologues* with his girl-friend and her mother. He was not uncomfortable or intimidated by this situation. This CMF has many female friends and greatly values their opinions.

C Curious Male/Female Strategies

These candidates are ideal mates for a female who also has balanced interests and maintains friendships with both sexes. Women who can enjoy watching a football game with a mate as well as the ballet can find these bonds mutually fulfilling. Men and women are clearly different and this individual is willing to learn about you.

Don't worry about his female friends. CMFs are more balanced because of friendships with the opposite sex. If you get jealous easily, you may damage the bond and then miss out on a wonderful connection. Try to evaluate the situation and understand the person better before walking away. CMF traits can actually be the basis for a foundation of mutual respect and lifelong commitment.

Curious Male/Female Questions

1. How do you feel about having a girlfriend who has male friendships?

2. Tell me about your female friends and interests that you share with them.

3. What types of interests do you think someone should share with his or her mate?

DGI—Dysfunctional Guy with Issues

Dysfunctional Guy with Issues Definition

A Dysfunctional Guy with Issues (DGI) is most likely a 35+male who has never been married. Everyone is dysfunctional to a degree, but there may be more baggage if someone has not made a commitment by 35. DGIs are often resistant to partnerships and can be frustrating candidates if you are seeking someone to go the distance. This definition is a broad and general one based solely on age and commitment history. You will need to dig deeper to determine the complexity level of the dysfunction.

Dysfunctional Guy with Issues Example

I dated a successful journalist who, at 47 years old, appeared to have it all together on the surface. This DGI was charismatic with a great career and solid friendships. He was intelligent and witty with a full list of manly and cultural interests.

He told me about several long-term relationships in his past and it seemed odd that he never had made a marriage commitment. In one case, he dated a woman for two years, found an apartment to share with her, and then asked her to move out after just a few months. He never explained why, but I tried to overlook these issues because I was nuts about him.

We spent an intense four-day weekend away together and it was magical. His eyes were teary when I left, and it seemed to me that a powerful connection had been established. But instead of taking the relationship to the next level, this DGI began to make up excuses why it would not work and basically backed away.

D When I looked deeper, I found that he had a non-traditional family with many divorces, stepsiblings and half-siblings. However, he had a good relationship with his mother. I took the latter as a positive sign, but clearly there were too many hidden issues. After an agonizing year spent trying to make the relationship happen, I finally waved the surrender flag. In an email, he apologized for being "less than a gentleman," said I deserved better, and wished me the best of luck.

Dysfunctional Guy with Issues Strategies

When you come across a 35+male who has never made a real commitment, give serious thought to looking elsewhere. If you decide to proceed anyway, ask questions about his relationship history and family dynamics to uncover any potential patterns. Avoid playing the caretaker and making up excuses for him because it can be exhausting with little pay-off. In addition, don't think that you can fix him because old habits are almost impossible to break at this age. Somebody else probably thought the same thing before you.

Perhaps he has just not met the right one. However, you will need to decide how much time you want to invest in a potentially unavailable candidate. I wasted a year.

Dysfunctional Guy with Issues LIFE Questions

1. What do you like to do when you are not working?

2. Can you describe your last important relationship?

3. Tell me why you have never been married.

ESS—Executive Search Seeker

Executive Search Seeker Definition

Executive Search Seekers (ESS) are professional men who only want career-oriented women. These men are obsessed with their own work, and need a companion who can understand this passion and is equally driven. ESSs have a myopic definition of their search parameters. They tend to be over-achievers and require similar traits in a mate. Because ESSs are clear in their expectations they can be a great match for success-driven women.

Executive Search Seeker Example

I exchanged emails with an ESS candidate whom I met via Internet dating. We later spoke on the phone for over an hour before our first live encounter. He played a leadership role for a very successful management-consulting firm and made it clear that this job was his life. This ESS typically worked over seventy hours per week. This prospect was direct in his requirement for a companion who could understand his lifestyle and career focus. We exchanged experiences working with Fortune 1000 clients and discovered that we shared similar management philosophies.

At the end of this lengthy introductory call, we decided to meet the following evening during his airport layover in Los Angeles en route back to his home in Orlando, Florida. In preparation for our meeting, he gave me homework. This ESS asked me to analyze his company's web site and be prepared to give him feedback. Because of my e-commerce experience creating web site content, I accepted the challenge.

E During our brief meeting, the candidate dominated the conversation with the results of his client meetings that day. He was extremely wound up and passionate about his work. When it came time for my web site analysis, the ESS was disappointed that I did not have more comments on the graphics. At the end of this 30-minute meeting, he gave me a follow-up assignment that consisted of more web site reviews.

When I left the airport, my cell phone rang. It was the ESS. He said that he enjoyed our brief meeting and was looking forward to receiving the results of my second quiz. I felt exhausted by the encounter and knew there was no chemistry. This guy was just too intense for me.

Executive Search Seeker Strategies

For a career woman, there are many benefits to sharing your business passions with a mate. However, an ESS can be very self-focused and too absorbed in his work to create a mutually beneficial bond. Because women are multi-taskers, they can usually do a better job balancing career and relationship needs.

An ESS male may create an emotionally lop-sided partnership because he is unable to separate from his work. Evaluate the dynamics of the relationship and decide if your ESS provides complementary traits or is simply a drain on your energy.

Executive Search Seeker LIFE Questions

1. Can you tell me about your female friends and their careers?

2. How important is it to you that your female mate has a successful career?

3. What information do you like to discuss with a partner about your work?

FE—Fitness Extremist

Fitness Extremist Definition

A Fitness Extremist (FE) is obsessed with regular workouts and healthy living. If he does not exercise at least five times a week, the FE is disappointed in himself and feels his muscles turning into fat. His diet consists primarily of vegetables and protein, and it will be almost impossible to break this regimen.

An FE is so absorbed by this healthy lifestyle that he most likely needs a woman with similar workout and diet routines. FEs are totally body conscious and will probably demand the same focus from their mate.

Fitness Extremist Example

One of my 30-something girlfriends dated a 41-year-old Fitness Extremist, who was a professional bike racer. His entire life revolved around a strictly defined diet, eating schedules, and regular prolonged workouts.

There was no breaking this routine. If she wanted to go away with him for the weekend, he needed to be able to access a gym and continue his extreme diet. Whenever she found herself enjoying a piece of tiramisu, she was always alone and feeling guilty. She also felt that her own body never met his expectations.

Her FE's diet prescribed no wheat, sugar or carbohydrates. His favorite foods were sushi and skinless chicken. Some of her favorite foods were at the other extreme—and included pasta, ice cream, and Captain Crunch.

F After months of trying to make the relationship work, she recognized that this FE was not a candidate worth pursuing. She could never match his fitness obsession, and did not want to live with the pressure and guilt of always coming up short of his expectations.

Fitness Extremist Strategies

Fitness Extremists can be great mates if you have similar workout and diet goals. If you enjoy regular aerobic activities and monitor your eating habits, the FE may be the man for you.

Alternatively, if you are not an FE, be honest with yourself and walk away. This relationship will only frustrate you. You will drive yourself crazy by feeling a self-imposed pressure to eat and exercise the FE way.

If this FE is the man of your dreams and you want to pursue a relationship, ask him to share his fitness expectations for a partner. He may surprise you. If he seems less demanding than your perception, set a timeframe to test the relationship out. Periodic reality checks will give you opportunities to make go/no-go decisions.

Fitness Extremist LIFE Questions

1. What type of diet do you think is important?

2. Tell me more about how often you workout and the importance of these sessions.

3. What parts of your health regimen do you like to share with a mate?

GWO—Guy with Offspring

Guy with Offspring Definition

Meeting a Guy with Offspring (GWO) happens frequently today with the soaring divorce rates. Obviously, these candidates are men with children from a previous relationship. The GWOs will vary greatly in terms of time commitments to their family. Some parents share custody so the children stay regularly at his home. Other GWOs have children who live in different cities and only see them during holidays and on special occasions. The relationship with the former partner also has a major impact on parent-child dynamics and interactions.

Guy with Offspring Example

My 35-year-old friend married someone with a 2-year-old daughter from a previous marriage. This GWO was extremely dedicated to his father-daughter relationship. In this case, my friend found it was easier dating a GWO with a young child versus a teenager. However, an irrational ex-spouse complicated their interactions.

In this case, the ex-spouse initially made it almost impossible for her husband to maintain a healthy bond with his child. The mother was a control freak holding most of the emotional trump cards, which created great heartache for my friend and the GWO.

My friend had to be very supportive of her GWO husband due to a difficult ex-spouse. She was flexible with her time and commitments. Initially, the newlyweds were never certain when a visit would be allowed. As a result of her willingness to openly address the situation and support the GWO, the experience has enhanced their marriage by bringing them closer together.

G Guy with Offspring Strategies

Anyone dealing with a GWO needs to ask herself difficult questions about the impact of a child on the relationship. In order to be fair to the Man Candidate and his child, be honest with your answers. If you have kids and know the routine, you are in familiar territory and better equipped to deal with the myriad aspects of custody. If you do not have kids, evaluate the relationship and whether it is worth your time and emotion to invest further in this GWO.

Beware of the GWO who feels guilt for not spending enough time with his children. You may end up feeling that your relationship is in competition with the parent-child bond. If you find the GWO always canceling dates at the last minute to be with his children, you should reconsider whether this relationship makes you feel good.

Whenever children are involved, there is a required level of compromise. Determine whether you can handle the level needed by the GWO. Ideally, you want to find a mate who can balance relationships with you and the child. Continuous open and honest dialogue can walk you through the issues and make the bond stronger.

Guy with Offspring LIFE Questions

1. Can you tell me more about your relationship with your children?

2. What role does each parent play in raising the children?

3. Can you describe the dynamics of your relationship with their mother?

HGG—Hello Goodbye Guy

Hello Goodbye Guy Definition

The Hello Goodbye Guy (HGG) will convince you that he is genuinely interested in moving forward at first. You make connections with him easily, and he seems like a strong prospect. The Hello Goodbye Guy is very polite, complimentary, and leaves you with the impression that there is a future.

However, after only a few encounters, he suddenly vanishes with no explanation, leaving you checking your deodorant, neuroses, sex appeal and everything else to find out what went wrong. HGGs will avoid all future contact, leaving you blind-sided and baffled.

Hello Goodbye Guy Examples

My first example of a Hello Goodbye Guy is from an Internet dating experience. There are many HGGs on the Internet dating scene who will email you back and forth diligently at first, ask you personal questions and lead you to believe that you have made a meaningful connection.

This guy asked me to tell him about why I moved to California, whether my divorce was amicable (which it was), and to describe details about my family relationships. He was forthcoming with answers to the same personal questions from me. After a week of openly sharing long emails regarding family values and relationship histories, he suddenly stopped writing with no explanation. His disappearance left me feeling empty and confused.

Another example of a Hello Goodbye Guy was someone whom I met through mutual friends. I probably trusted him more because of the association. This 44-year-old candidate made special efforts to find my

H phone number, was a complete gentleman, and immediately scheduled a follow-up date. We had four awesome dates with what seemed to be mutual mental and physical attractions. I was convinced that we were heading into something with great potential. After a few days with no contact, I started to wonder. After a few weeks of additional silence, I realized he was a HGG and knocked him off my pre-conceived pedestal.

Hello Goodbye Guy Strategies

Even if friends introduce you, take it slowly in the beginning with any candidate. Interview him thoroughly and avoid making assumptions too soon. Because HGGs are often charmers, it is not always easy to pace the emotional and physical interactions. Control yourself to protect your ego and maintain your dignity.

If you are fooled by an HGG, use the experience as a learning opportunity and don't beat yourself up over it. Avoid taking it personally because it is not your issue. HGGs can be slick masters of deception. Next time, remind yourself that first impressions can be misleading. If he sounds too good to be true, there is probably something hidden behind door number three. Take time to assess the candidates and avoid making hasty assumptions.

Hello Goodbye Guy LIFE Questions

1. What is the longest relationship in your past?

2. What aspects do you enjoy about being in a relationship?

3. How long do you think it takes to determine if someone might be "the one" for you?

IP—Internet Psycho

Internet Psycho Definition

Internet Psychos (IPs) are rare and dangerous men who seek thrills by antagonizing women they meet through the latest technology. Extreme bizarre behavior is common among these men, and they will invariably shock and disappoint you. IPs take advantage of the anonymity of Internet dating to fool and victimize women who don't exercise extreme caution.

Internet Psycho Examples

If you receive an email that resembles this one, check to see if you can block the email address, and hit delete because you know you are dealing with an IP: "I would like to undress that sexy body of yours by your fireplace, rub strawberries all over you, and…"

Some IPs are less obvious so try to avoid the mistakes that I made while Internet dating. My second example is frightening and I definitely learned a lesson about never giving out your home phone number to strangers over the Internet. I received an email from an Internet dating candidate who was a 38-year-old actor living in Beverly Hills. His photos were impressive studio black and whites. His essay responses were direct and witty, which sparked my interest. His first email was a one-liner that said, "I liked your profile, send me your phone number." Initially, I responded by asking more questions. His second email response asked again for my phone number. I had a weak moment and made the mistake of giving it to him.

During the first call, he asked me, "When are you coming over?" I told him that I was not and that he should go to the next person on his list.

I The IP continued to persist by stating that he did not do the "Starbucks thing" and that I would have to do that with other guys. I continued to tell him no thank you. He then had the nerve to comment, "Well if you change your mind let me know because I have four or five women who come over every week." I remained calm, giving him no reaction, and quickly got off the call. Fortunately, I never heard from this Internet Psycho again.

The third IP example was less obvious and surprised me. While I had been warned to watch out for IPs, I still unwittingly managed to set up a date with a crazy man. I exchanged at least ten emails with him, shared photos, and we discussed our career and personal interests. He seemed like a stable divorced father who was a 44-year-old professor at a top-notch university where several of my friends attended business school. When he invited me to dinner via email, I accepted the invitation without bothering to check the location or question whether I should have confirmed on the phone.

As I approached the restaurant, it was clear that I was in fact nowhere near my Santa Monica bubble. It was a bleak neighborhood with bars on windows and doors. I repeated my Los Angeles mantra of KIT (Keep it Together) in my head and proceeded with caution. The IP date was for 7:00 P.M. and when he didn't show by 7:20 P.M., I was a little concerned. I tried calling him and left a message stating that perhaps Friday night traffic was delaying him and asked him to call me. By 7:45 P.M., I decided it was time for my exit.

The next day I received an apology email from this IP with the lamest excuse. The IP stated that he was not used to meeting for dates without talking on the phone with a candidate prior to the engagement. He also made an obnoxiously weird comment about "getting back to my ski trip and broken ankle." I didn't have a clue what that meant, and I responded with a short email stating that his apology was not accepted and that I felt sorry for anyone who encountered him. How would he feel if someone stood up his daughter in a gang neighborhood?

Internet Psycho Strategies

Watch out for Internet Psycho warning signs when you are setting up dates online. Never give out your last name or phone number until you have had a first meeting as a precautionary measure. If the psycho is obvious, see if you can block his email address immediately.

I also recommend at least one phone conversation with Internet dating candidates prior to any meeting, to help you detect wackos. Remember that you need to ask the guy for his phone number and use Caller ID blocking (*67) when you place the call. If you sense during the call that you're dealing with an IP, run as you would from a telemarketer from hell. Avoid all future contact with this individual.

If you have a persistent harassment problem, you may also want to consider other security precautions or to contact your local law enforcement authorities without delay.

Internet Psycho LIFE Questions

1. Tell me about your Internet dating experience.

2. Have you met anyone that you liked through Internet dating?

3. What steps do you usually take when pursuing someone via Internet dating?

JJ—Justifying Juggler

Justifying Juggler Definition

Justifying Jugglers (JJ) date as a many women as possible at the same time—and do not even try to hide it. The JJ will try to convince you that his juggling act is acceptable behavior. These men love women and fill their lives with multiple relationships. The JJ is extremely self-focused and narcissistic. He truly believes that everyone should love him and has no concept of commitment.

Justifying Juggler Example

My 32-year-old girlfriend dated a dance instructor with pronounced JJ characteristics. He was incredibly charming and possessed an exceptional understanding of women. This 36-year-old JJ was also extremely sexy and oozed charisma. He had the gift that caused females to tolerate or at least overlook his unconventional lifestyle.

She knew this JJ had dated many other students from the dance studio, but it just didn't matter. Everyone adored him and accepted his behavior. My friend felt safe as long as she did not get emotionally involved. She knew the game, and had no qualms about his intentions. There was zero chance of commitment or change in his behavior.

She saw the Justifying Juggler every day in dance studio classes. He was extremely passionate about every aspect of women. The JJ made all females feel special with continuous and sincere compliments. Even the ones that were less than physically stunning he made feel like goddesses as long as they were good dancers.

The Justifying Juggler made no effort to hide his attractions to, affections for and appreciation of other women. As a result, my friend had to accept

his preference for multiple partners. Their relationship accom-
modated his world. She enjoyed their time together, kept her
expectations in check, and does not regret her experience.

Justifying Juggler Strategies

If you can handle a relationship with no commitment, the Justifying
Juggler can be an ego boost and a ton of fun. However, because you are
seeking a lifetime mate, there is probably little room or desire to entertain these charismatic charmers.

Evaluate your personal needs and preferences carefully to avoid situations that can be time wasters. Avoid misinterpreting his intentions. You
are kidding yourself if you think the JJ will suddenly have a change of
heart and lifestyle on your account.

The Justifying Juggler will never be "the one." Because of his passion for
women, he will never settle for one partner. These men are not potential
life-mates. If you decide that you cannot resist a JJ, set realistic expectations and make sure it is a win-win situation.

Justifying Juggler LIFE Questions

1. What are you seeking in the dating arena?

2. Have you ever fallen for more than one person at a time and
   what happened?

3. Do you think a monogamous relationship is possible today?

KOF—Keeper of the Fire

Keeper of the Fire Definition

The Keeper of the Fire (KOF) is a romantic who will perpetually maintain interest by intermittently stoking the flames with surprise acts of adoration. These men will regularly remind you of their devotion. They enjoy making an effort and gain satisfaction from making you smile. The KOF does not need to spend a lot money to sustain sparks. KOFs will find creative and often inexpensive ways to keep the fire going.

Keeper of the Fire Examples

My 38-year-old friend is dating a textbook example of a Keeper of the Fire. He brings her a gift every time they go out, which adds surprise and sparks to their relationship. The KOF gifts are not extravagant, but show great thought. For example, he gave her a CD of his favorite music. Another night he brought her a gift certificate for a massage after she had just managed avoiding a lay-off at work. This romantic wanted to recognize that she had had a tough day. His kind gesture had a powerful impact.

Another KOF example was the 39-year-old artist that I dated in Washington D.C. He showed his appreciation through acts of kindness and little gestures. For example, while I was on a business trip for a month, he cleaned my apartment, including scrubbing the bathroom tiles. This KOF also loved cooking dinner on the grill for me on summer Sundays. He left me cute notes and cards, while moving very slowly with the physical interactions. He communicated his preference for building a loving long-term relationship prior to having sex. This KOF was a serious contender, but I let him get away for other reasons.

Keeper of the Fire Strategies

K

KOFs are great romantics and excellent matches for women seeking a sincere partner. At this stage in life, it is time to evaluate the core and not be dazzled by the resume. It's important find someone who appreciates you, and attitude is key. You should be tired of playing guessing games with effortless men.

If you are fortunate to find a KOF, let him spoil you. Don't feel that you need to return every gesture either. Instead, look for opportunities to surprise him when the timing is right.

Even if you feel uncomfortable with a KOF, take a second look. Be open to his acts of romance and carefully evaluate the potential before you end the relationship. KOFs are not easy to find and can bring you a lifetime of little joys. After the sexual passion fades, the KOF keeps the fire burning with his constant reminders that you are "the one."

Keeper of the Fire LIFE Questions

1. How would you define romance?

2. How do you think married couples keep the flame alive over the years?

3. Can you describe your idea of a romantic evening to me?

LS—Lost Soul

Lost Soul Definition

Lost Souls (LS) are primarily disconnected from others. They have shields that hide their emotions, and their history includes few intimate relationships. The LS rarely communicates his personal thoughts. Instead, the conversation is focused on events and unemotional facts because he is really not interested in your feelings and could not get in touch with his own if he used a pick and shovel.

These men may impress you with business success, but their career achievements are rooted in the fact that they find more comfort in the office where it is taboo to express emotions. Off the clock, the LS is often alone or with other male friends. Males are less likely to discuss feelings, so their company creates a safe haven for the LS. The LS is often in denial of his disconnected status because he doesn't see a need to build a meaningful partnership in the first place.

Lost Soul Example

My girlfriend dated a 46-year-old actor who was very successful on the set. Off-stage with this LS, however, she saw a different picture. This LS only talked about his work, music, and world news. He avoided all conversations that disclosed feelings. While he is brilliant, this LS has trouble maintaining interpersonal relationships.

When she asked him what he liked to do during his free time, his response was, "I like to watch a lot of TV." She thought he was kidding until they spent a weekend together in his environment. This LS also was also a manly man who enjoyed fencing, watching NASCAR races and drinking with his buddies.

It did not take long before she decided this individual was a Lost Soul. He was incapable of emotional intimacy, and his issues were not about her. This LS had a record of partnership avoidance and indicated no signs of changing in the near future.

L

Lost Soul Strategies

I cannot stress enough how quickly you should sprint from a Lost Soul. Ask questions about his relationship history to uncover this pattern early. Watch for the warning signs and be honest about his ability to have a relationship with any woman. If he seems withdrawn and has never had a long-term involvement with anyone, these red flags should immediately steer you to run in the opposite direction and start screaming, "WARNING, WARNING, DO NOT ENTER!"

Because the LS can be in his career prime, avoid being misled by business achievements. Don't try to force the LS to emotionally connect with you. Trying to change an LS will only bring frustration and heartache. Remind yourself that you deserve more from any relationship. Move on with confidence that your soul mate is out there.

Lost Soul LIFE Questions

1. Tell me more about your family dynamics.

2. How does your family like to spend holidays?

3. Tell me about your friends and how often you get to see them.

MBA—Married But Available

Married But Available Definition

Married But Available (MBA) suitors are married men with no plans for shucking their legal bonds even though they are willing to have an affair or relationship with you. These players are very open about their intentions and are content to let you decide if you want to accept their terms. Depending on your culture, mindset and value systems, responses to MBA proposals can vary.

Married But Available Examples

Here are two examples of MBAs, one European and the other American:

The first example is a 44-year-old film buyer from Holland who was extremely open about his desire to have a fling with me. I met this MBA at a trendy film industry party in Los Angeles. We danced to '70s disco music for 30 minutes before I noticed his wedding band. The chemistry connection was clearly there, but my conservative upbringing prevented all thoughts of an affair. He tried to convince me that his definition of marriage was different from mine and allowed him to have a fling with impunity. This MBA wanted to leave the party with me and was quite persistent. I maintained my ground and he did not understand why.

While European men tend to be more open about affairs, MBAs are usually not as public in the United States. My 37-year-old married friend in Los Angeles, who frequents a gym three days a week, provided more prime examples to me. She has developed associations with many of the other gym regulars. Married men openly share stories about and pictures of their families with her, all the while dropping hints that despite their marital ties, they are interested in her. These men often make insinuations indicating that an affair would be acceptable.

"Being monogamous is difficult when you are married," said one MBA to my friend. This MBA asked her to stop by his bar for a drink. Another MBA asked about the status of her marriage. She responds to such thinly veiled invitations to infidelity by joking her way out it. Despite her defenses, these domestic MBAs are relentless in their pursuit.

Married But Available Strategies

There are several questions you need to ask yourself when dealing with an MBA. The first is whether you are interested. The second question is whether you want to take a risk and deal with the consequences of getting involved with someone who technically and legally belongs to another woman.

If you are interested in a fling, remember that this MBA is not leaving his wife. The encounter will only provide temporary entertainment and can result in long-term heartache. Avoid building an ongoing relationship with an MBA. You might waste years dreaming about him leaving his wife while he enjoys the best of both worlds. If you must go there, keep it short and stay detached.

Your best bet is to forget all thoughts about MBAs. These men are trouble and will only complicate your life. MBAs will steal valuable time and emotions that could be spent looking for Mr. Right.

Married But Available LIFE Questions

1. Tell me about your marriage and whether you are happy.

2. What is your definition of marriage?

3. Have you considered leaving your wife and why?

NN—Nourishing Nester

Nourishing Nester Definition

The Nourishing Nester (NN) prefers spending quality time at home with a mate and will feed your soul with good will. These men thrive on building their nest. NNs are content being in this environment with their small circle of close friends and loved ones. These candidates would rather be with you one-on-one than in a large crowd. Nourishing Nesters tend to be family-oriented even if they are not married.

Nourishing Nester Example

Through an Internet dating service, I met a Nourishing Nester (NN) that was a 49-year-old TV producer. All of our dates were one-on-one. On our third date, he invited me for a full tour of his home. This NN proudly explained the meaning of his photographs and paintings during the visit. On our fifth date, he invited me over for sandwiches and the Super Bowl. He made it clear that his preference was to be at home rather than in a crowd for this major sporting event.

This NN was very close to his family and spoke warmly about them frequently. There were pictures everywhere of his parents and siblings. He took great interest in my personal well-being and my family. When I hurt my back, he called every day to check on me. When my brother came to Los Angeles, he invited us to visit his castle. He made it clear from the beginning that he wanted a relationship with me. All of his actions were directed towards building a nest with me. Unfortunately, I was distracted by stronger feelings for other potential partners at the time, which ultimately cut off this NN's path.

Nourishing Nester Strategies

$$\boxed{\mathbf{N}}$$

NNs can be great long-term partners and potential fathers. These relationships can be fulfilling because you know the NN is sincere. These men will be there for you in good times and bad, which is exactly what you want in a lifetime mate.

Consider whether his lifestyle works with your personality. If you need constant large group activities, this mate may clash with you. However, if you want to create a family nest, the parties can wait. When you grow old and gray, the NN will stay by your side when the crowds will be long gone.

If you are not ready for a NN, be honest with him. He will appreciate the candor, and it will enable him to devote his nurturing efforts towards finding someone who more closely mirrors his priorities.

Nourishing Nester LIFE Questions

1. Tell me more about where you live.

2. Would you rather spend time at home or out in the crowds?

3. Tell me about a time when someone in your family got sick and you were able to help them.

OO—Over-Achiever Obsessor

Over-Achiever Obsessor Definition

The Over-Achiever Obsessor (OO) has spent his entire adult life adding medals to his trophy case. He displays them proudly on his resume for the world to notice. His primary focus has been on collecting achievements versus building a marital relationship. OOs take great pride in earning advanced degrees and steadily moving up the corporate ladder with promotions. OOs tend to get a wake-up call in their 40s when they suddenly see a need to find a romantic partner. Although these OOs will never give up their obsession with career success, they are genuinely seeking a mate to fill the one gap in their life.

Over-Achiever Obsessor Example

Briefly, I dated a 39-year-old OO, who later became a good friend and confidant. This OO has an MBA, JD, and a Masters in Technology from Ivy-League schools. He has a long list of career achievements to complement his education and now sits on the boards of over ten companies. Because of his tremendous career success, he is also very comfortable financially. He has extensively traveled the world and is now seriously seeking a mate.

This OO started approaching his search with the same intensity of his career achievements. Similar to a requirements document, this OO created a checklist in his mind for a suitable mate. He first contacted friends and then used his industry networking resources. In addition, he took advantage of Internet dating sites. He set up multiple dates with women in the same week for one-hour coffee talks similar to the way he scheduled business meetings.

Several times he felt as if he had met "the one" only to discover that this hasty approach was pushing him to force a match. After jumping into two

short-winded serious relationships, this OO slowed down and
began taking time for more upfront dialogs about partnership
expectations and dug deeper than his checklist. As a result, he found a
potential life partner. He has been dating her for over six months and I
hear wedding bells.

O

Over-Achiever Obsessor Strategies

OOs tend to put their business goals before personal relationships so
you should be careful getting involved with one. You will not be the top
priority unless he has reached a personal turning point where seeking a
mate is just as important as his career.

Even with a commitment to make a relationship work, the OO will continue to show overwhelming passion for his work. If you don't need a
lot of attention and are a good listener, you may be very OO compatible. These partners can provide excitement and financial stability.

In addition, the Over-Achiever Obsessor can make adjustments to find
room for a relationship. Evaluate if the OO is Emotionally Ready for a
partner. Take advantage of his goal-setting tendencies by using interview questions that uncover his relationship expectations.

In addition, if you are an OO, this match will either be ideal or a complete clash. Carefully assess the dynamics to determine the likelihood of
complimentary mindsets. Some OOs will want a companion who can
relate to the demands of their passions. Others will want to come home
to a work-free dinner conversation.

Over-Achiever Obsessor LIFE Questions

1. Tell me about your personal and career goals.

2. Tell me how you balance your career with personal interests and
   family.

3. Tell me about your biggest personal achievement and why it was
   important to you?

PTS—*Post Traumatic Soul*

Post Traumatic Soul Definition

Post Traumatic Souls (PTS) are males who have been shaken by a recent life-altering event. The experience makes such a significant impact that the individual starts re-evaluating his priorities. The PTS may be withdrawn and usually limits his interactions to a close circle of friends. The pivotal event may be the loss of a loved-one, a physical injury or illness, or some other mental hardship.

Post Traumatic Soul Examples:

The first and most dramatic example of a PTS that I have encountered was someone I met while stranded in NYC during the week of September 11th. I met this 37-year-old rock star through mutual friends during a dinner. We immediately connected and consoled each other emotionally. While the rest of our group wanted to dance all night after dinner, this PTS asked me to join him for a drink in an uncrowded bar. He shared his story with me. This PTS was concerned about his father who worked at a school across from the World Trade Center. While his father turned out to be all right, the rock star was emotionally shaken and upset about going back on the road for another band tour with the looming fear of another terrorist attack.

After returning to Los Angeles, this PTS went on tour in Asia. He called me from Melbourne, Sydney, Auckland and Tokyo. We talked for hours. Because he could not keep the time zones straight and it was important to stay connected, I accepted his calls even at 3:00 A.M. This PTS was constantly watching CNN and alternating phone calls between his parents and me. He told me that it was important for him to stay in contact with those close to him no matter where his job took him. This PTS clearly was going through a life-changing event and reached out to me for support.

The second example of a PTS is a 40-year-old lawyer I dated in Washington D.C. About four months into the relationship, he received a life-altering call that his mother had been suddenly killed in a car accident in Chile. I immediately left my new job to join his family who were in serious shock.

The PTS was visibly devastated and it changed the dynamics of our relationship. Suddenly, I became more of counselor and tried to help him deal with this tragedy. While I consider myself a good listener and loyal friend, the PTS demands continued to be a drain and ultimately ended the relationship a year later. He was a good guy, but our timing was just not right.

Post Traumatic Soul Strategies

When you find a life partner or long-term mate, you will eventually face life-altering events together that can make or break the relationship. These changes will eventually result in a relationship re-evaluation. Consider the strength of the bond and your emotional status. Look at how the relationship dynamic has changed and the potential long-term impact of the situation.

Without open communication, the relationship is over. You need answers to difficult questions. This dialogue will help you identify ways to support the PTS versus push you apart. Recognize your limitations and do not take the PTS actions personally during this period. You may even want to set a personal timeframe for how long you can continue in this relationship and then see if the dynamics begin to improve. Unfortunately, the situation may be out of your control and the relationship cannot survive the tragedy.

P However, these situations can also strengthen a bond. Carefully consider how the PTS responds to you and whether he lets you help him. If he demonstrates trust and respect in you, these can be great signs for a potential life partner. You may want to support the PTS through the hardship. In the end, you will be a stronger couple with greater chances of long-term success.

If you encounter a PTS on your dating journey, be careful to give yourself regular reality checks on the situation. While you want to be a supporter, you need to be honest with yourself regarding the impact this dynamic is playing on your life. These situations are not easy and require great care and grace. It's all about finding the right balance, and if you can't, knowing when to cut your losses when dating a PTS.

Post Traumatic Soul LIFE Questions

1. Have you ever suffered a great loss? Can you tell me what happened?

2. How did you cope with your loss?

3. What stages did you experience when you suffered your loss?

QP—Questionnaire Perfectionist

Questionnaire Perfectionist Definition

The Questionnaire Perfectionist (QP) has a defined list of mate requirements. He is seeking an ideal partner who matches 100 percent of his criteria. While some QPs will leave a small margin for differences, these men tend to reject anything that is not close to perfection. Their questionnaire details will vary depending on what is important to the QP. Some critical checklist items may include age, politics, religion, money, priorities, hair color, height, weight, fitness and hobbies.

Questionnaire Perfectionist Example

I married a QP at 30, who is now no longer my husband. Initially, I was blinded by the strong mutual physical attraction. We were so in love that details were never discussed. However, I soon found out about his list of requirements for a mate. When we first dated, we overlooked core priorities because our time was spent sharing mutual interests in biking, hiking, and the arts.

Once we started living together, the QP began to reveal critical needs that he desired from me as his mate. His list was non-negotiable. For example, the QP told me that he wanted to go camping at least once a month with me. As a compromise, I offered to go camping twice per year and encouraged him to go more often with his friends. However, he would not accept these terms. While this issue may sound trivial, it was very important to him and became a serious conflict. When he wanted to go camping for our honeymoon, I should have recognized this extreme interest.

This QP also expected me to spend every Saturday at home working on the house with him. Because I worked all week, I wanted to play on this day off. I had no interest in painting and scrubbing the house. This conflict in priorities and interests created another major relationship clash.

Q As the QP expectations grew, we ended up in counseling. We each made a list of our needs, but he was not willing to compromise. His demands were black and white and any proposed shade of gray was not acceptable to him. The QP requirements created so many roadblocks that there was no other choice but to part ways.

Questionnaire Perfectionist Strategies

As soon as a relationship begins to get serious start asking some detailed questions to uncover whether this potential mate is a Questionnaire Perfectionist. Once you understand his expectations, it is easier to determine whether you can fulfill any non-negotiable needs.

If you are lucky, you may discover that the QP shares your priorities and interests. In this case, you are fortunate to have found a match.

Alternatively, if the QP reveals expectations that you cannot meet, don't overlook the potential long-term issues that may result. QPs will not give up their list, and it is hopeless to try to change them. If you ignore the importance of his requirements, you may end up divorced or trapped in a lifetime of conflict.

However, if you are comfortable making changes to meet the QP needs, proceed cautiously without giving up your own sense of self. Test compromises and take periodic reality checks to make sure that it is a mutually beneficial partnership.

Questionnaire Perfectionist LIFE Questions

1. Tell me what you consider to be a perfect match for you.

2. Tell me about the aspects of a relationship that you think can and cannot be compromised.

3. What qualities in a candidate have been deal-breakers in the past and why?

RR—Relentless Renter

Relentless Renter Definition

Relentless Renters (RR) are men who want to have a relationship and will even live with you long-term, but will never make the ultimate commitment of marriage. The RR is monogamous and a good partner, but has a genuine fear of lifetime agreements. Relentless Renters prefer to have all the benefits of a relationship without the legal bonds.

Relentless Renter Example

A girlfriend of mine has been dating a doctor in his mid-40s for a significant period of time, and there are still no signs of wedding bells. His plans are as clear as the scribbling on his prescription pad. This Relentless Renter has a pattern of long-term, non-marital relationships.

Prior to his relationship with my friend, he dated someone for seven years and never popped the question. As in this RR's prior relationship, my friend lives with him, shares pets, and holds joint bank accounts. They are both very involved with each other's families. In her view, this Relentless Renter is faithful, giving, supportive and a good partner.

However, my friend is now almost 40 and wants to be married and have children. She has discussed her intentions with him, but he continues to avoid the ultimate leap. The couple has been together for over a year, and she is planning to leave him if the situation is unchanged at the two-year milestone.

R | Relentless Renter Strategies

Even though the Relentless Renter is a committed partner, recognize that these men will steer clear of marriage proposals at all costs. Avoid giving ultimatums because you will lose.

However, it is important to ask questions early to uncover this preference and evaluate your personal needs. If you are in your 30s or 40s and want children, RRs will only delay meeting your goal.

On the other hand, keep in mind that many people are now replacing traditional marriages with this modern version of a long-term commitment. If you are comfortable with this progressive partnership, your RR may be a good match. Many women who have been previously married might prefer a Relentless Renter versus the potential of another divorce.

Relentless Renter LIFE Questions

1. Have you ever lived with a partner? What aspects did you enjoy about the arrangement?

2. What is the longest time that you have lived with someone and why did it end?

3. Do you believe in the concept of marriage?

SG—Social Guru

Social Guru Definition

The Social Guru (SG) is the life of the party. He thrives on social inter-action with diverse groups of people. The SG likes to be the center of attention, and feeds his ego off the crowd's responses. He prefers to have a special someone to be on his wing. These individuals can be great diplomats with high energy and confidence. SGs can also be very enter-taining and have a great zest for life.

Social Guru Example

My 30-something girlfriend lived with a Social Guru who just turned 43. He is the CEO of a dot.com who thrives on social interactions. He is always organizing group activities. This Social Guru frequently calls friends to join him for bike rides on the beach, bowling, movies and dinners.

This SG enjoys meeting new faces and encourages his close friends to invite strangers to these gatherings. He likes learning about other people and always asks many questions to gain knowledge about their experiences. During these activities, this SG loves being the cruise direc-tor, shares amusing tales, and often facilitates the discussion.

In contrast, my friend prefers quality time alone or with small groups. She found it exhausting to be his wing partner. She is intellectual and enjoys reading books versus spending time with strangers. Her life con-sists of graduate studies, daily walks with her black lab, and yoga.

As a result of these different preferences, they both learned to find a balance between social activities and quality time. He cut back on his frequency of organizing events. She made an effort to participate when

S he planned a gathering. Eventually, however, other issues intruded to end the relationship. Because they genuinely care about each other, they continue to maintain a friendship.

Social Guru Strategies

If you enjoy meeting people and do not need to be the center of attention in a group, Social Gurus can add fun and enthusiasm to your life. As long as you communicate your need for one-on-one timeouts, a relationship foundation can be built for a win-win situation. You can create a happy balance with this mutual understanding and compromise.

However, if you shy away from social settings, this relationship may be a struggle even with the foundation. Consider the SG's needs carefully and recognize that this interaction is essential for him to feel whole. If you try to eliminate these group activities, it will only build resentment and damage the relationship.

If you happen to be a female Social Guru, there may be a clash with this potential mate. Evaluate whether you think your styles complement each other or create a competition for center stage.

Social Guru LIFE Questions

1. When you go to a party, do you tend to stay with your date or divide and conquer the crowd?

2. How much time do you spend at social gatherings versus one-on-one situations?

3. Do you enjoy being a crowd leader and why or why not?

TT—Tasmanian Traveler

Tasmanian Traveler Definition

The Tasmanian Traveler (TT) is always on the move. The TT constantly travels for business and pleasure. These men tend to be on an airplane at least once a week, and it is difficult to keep up with their itineraries. Although the TT may want a relationship, his time is consumed by this hectic agenda. Most TTs are out-going and open-minded. They can easily adapt to diverse groups in various settings.

Tasmanian Traveler Examples

The first example is a TT that I met through Internet dating. This 50-something man initially emailed me from Australia, and we started scheduling a visit during a planned stopover in Los Angeles. The TT was going to be in Los Angeles for a week before heading to Canada to see his children, and then eventually returning to his island home on Anguilla in the Caribbean. Although his agenda made me dizzy, I was seeking someone who was worldly so I stayed in the game.

After several email exchanges, he took it to the next Internet dating level by calling me from Australia. The TT explained that he writes novels, which allowed him to keep a fluid travel schedule. The conversation was upbeat with multiple mental connections, so we decided to meet in Los Angeles.

Over coffee, the mutual chemistry test was passed. We shared mutual passions for international travel and writing. This TT had been a hotel chain owner before picking up his pen full-time. When he sold his hotels, the deal included significant discounts for him everywhere he traveled. With that incentive, he liked to travel around the world at least once a year.

Needless to say, his travel schedule was insane. Connecting again with this TT became almost impossible. I also became suspicious that he had a woman in every port. I did not see any potential for a lifetime partner here and quickly bid "ta-ta" to this TT.

The second TT example had a less hectic domestic travel schedule and managed partner communications much better. My girlfriend dated a 40-year-old TT who owned a paper recycling business in Los Angeles. His passion for riding in steeplechase races took him back East weekly in the spring. Because they shared this hobby and both traveled frequently, there was a level of understanding that made this demanding schedule less of an issue for them.

Despite his travel whirlwinds, this second TT continued to be attentive and maintained a solid relationship. The couple was constantly in contact through modern technology such as email, cell phones, and Blackberries.

Tasmanian Traveler Strategies

Because Tasmanian Travelers have extreme tendencies, consider whether you want this type of relationship. Ask yourself if you can handle being separated often and whether you are comfortable being on your own. If you are independent and also enjoy traveling, the TT may be an ideal mate.

While you may prefer someone who comes home every night, you should not immediately eliminate the TT from consideration, because he can bring other qualities to the relationship that makes it worth being flexible. If you take advantage of modern technology to maintain communication, you will greatly increase your chances for success with a Tasmanian Traveler partner.

Tasmanian Traveler LIFE Questions

1. Tell me about your travel schedule.

2. How do you keep in touch with close friends and family while traveling?

3. Tell me about the importance of communications to you while on the road.

UA—Under-Estimated Ally

Under-Estimated Ally Definition

Most of us have had close male friends we never considered as potential lovers. The Under-Estimated Ally (UA) continually gives you his time and energy. He will sincerely be sensitive to your peaks and valleys. UAs will always be supportive in a crisis and are often viewed as big brother types. Sometimes it is difficult to tell if they have any love interest in you because they never ask for anything in return.

Under-Estimated Ally Example

My 30-year-old girlfriend had a 34-year-old UA in her life that she did not view as a future mate. She was dating someone else and it never crossed her mind that her UA could be "the one." When she broke up with her boyfriend, it was not long before she realized the importance of her tie to this Under-Estimated Ally.

He was supportive through the break-up and made her feel wonderful with ego-boosting comments. The UA told her that it was the ex-boyfriend's loss and she was better off without him. Throughout the entire transition period, he was genuinely concerned about her well-being. They spent hours together sharing meals, going for runs, and talking through her feelings.

After a few months, it dawned on her that her UA relationship was evolving beyond friendship. Neither of them had ever discussed his or her feelings for each other. She did not know how he would respond if the issue was raised but she decided to take the risk and share her thoughts with the UA. When she disclosed her feelings, he responded favorably and it was the beginning of a life-long partnership. They were married two years later and have now been together for more than five years.

Under-Estimated Ally Strategies

Don't underestimate the value of a male friend because he might just be "the one" for you. You could be spending a lot of time with a male companion and overlook this potential. Even if you have been friends for a long time with no sexual interaction, it doesn't mean that it could not develop into something more.

These UAs can be great lifetime candidates because the foundation is already there. The UA has been there for you through the good and bad times, which is what you want in a partner. He is reliable and sincerely cares about you. So what are you waiting for to make a move?

While you may be worried about ruining a friendship, if you have true feelings it is worth taking a chance. By notifying him that your interest has gone to a new level, you may be pleasantly surprised to find that the feeling is mutual. If not, the friendship should be strong enough to withstand your confession.

Under-Estimated Ally LIFE Questions

1. Can you tell me about any friendships that turned into a relationship? How did it work out?

2. Tell me why our friendship is important to you.

3. Have you ever thought about us as more than just good friends?

VV—Vacillating Vortex

Vacillating Vortex Definition

The Vacillating Vortex (VV) is completely unpredictable and emotionally charged. These men will pull you in psychologically and then suddenly change their tune like a yoyo. These candidates will persuade you that your relationship is meaningful and moving forward, and then, with no warning, suddenly hit the reset button and leave you confused. VVs are dangerous because they will keep changing their mind about how they feel about you. This "stop and go" approach is a mind twister.

Vacillating Vortex Example

Through mutual friends, I met a Vacillating Vortex (VV) who appeared to be charming and genuine. He was a 36-year-old artist who was visiting Los Angeles from San Francisco. There was a clear physical attraction and intellectual connection. We sat by the fireplace as a group until 2:00 A.M. sharing colorful stories that first evening.

After this visit, we began a long-distance phone relationship. The conversations immediately took a deep and personal tone. For example, this VV loved to write poetry and started sharing his writing with me right out of the gates. Initially, he called me ten times in the first week. The VV openly confessed that he was pleasantly surprised by our connection and was starting to "fancy me."

After this week of two-hour-plus nightly phone calls, I was convinced there was a potential relationship brewing. I had previously dated long-distance partners, but this one felt different because of the intensity and openness. We talked about our passions, family dynamics and what was important to us in life.

Following a month of intense conversations, he took it to a
new level by calling at odd times such as 4:00 A.M. (which never
happened again after I clarified that late night calls were not acceptable)
and once at 8:00 A.M. on a Sunday to see what I was like first thing in the
morning.

V

At this point, it seemed logical to have an in-person visit to see if our
rapport would evolve into any type of physical connection. These calls
were consuming great energy and I did not want to continue getting
more emotionally involved without any eye-to-eye contact.

When I explained that I did not want to continue these lengthy calls
without a planned live visit on the horizon, he initially responded favorably. We had already discussed getting together but never set a date.
Now this VV said he was investigating flights and would visit within two
weeks. But other obligations intervened. Every time we reset our date,
he would end up canceling for one reason or another. The calls continued, although I began accepting them on a less frequent basis.

Eventually, I received the "let's be friends" and "I can't handle long-distance" speeches. The VV explained that he wanted to continue our
phone chats and maintain a friendship without the pressures of a relationship. I explained that I had romantic feelings for him and was not
interested in another male friendship. I was disappointed and felt as if I
had been used to fill a void. While I felt a great loss, I knew the shut-
down was necessary for my own well-being.

Vacillating Vortex Strategies

If someone is emotionally inconsistent, recognize this approach as a
danger sign of a Vacillating Vortex. Limit your initial time, energy and
openness to avoid being drawn into potential emotional damage. You
may think the interactions are valuable and laying the groundwork for a

solid relationship only to later discover that the VV is on a different track.

When dealing with a Vacillating Vortex, setting boundaries will help you protect yourself. Take precautions with these fast trains and ask tough questions to test his genuineness. You do not need to be confrontational but can simply end calls sooner and remove the VV's tendency to corner you into answering personal questions.

As soon as you see sudden shifts in his emotional connectivity, look out. Gracefully bow out of VV interludes and do not look back.

Vacillating Vortex LIFE Questions

1. Tell me about friendships that are important to you.

2. Tell me about your feelings for me.

3. Do you consider me as a friend or are we building a romantic relationship?

WD—Wounded Divorcé

Wounded Divorcé Definition

Wounded Divorcés (WD) are typically men who have been so damaged by a previous marriage that they block out any possibility of a future partnership. There are usually two causes of this mindset: emotional trauma and/or financial loss. Emotional trauma can be caused by a sudden and unanticipated break-up. Alimony and settlement costs can create anger and resentment. In many WD cases, both causes are prevalent and build walls around these divorced male candidates.

Wounded Divorcé Examples

I never met so many WDs before I moved to California, where community property laws tend to make divorce ugly. I dated two WDs who were charismatic, worldly, and dynamic individuals. However, they were damaged goods and not emotionally available.

WD #1 was a 41-year-old who made it clear from the beginning that he thought marriage was a hoax. He was married for six years and now shared custody of his daughter. This movie producer was a self-employed entrepreneur who had been in the business for years. I was completely blinded by his charisma and love for life, and new to the WD game.

This WD told me he was financially damaged because his income was at a peak at the time of his divorce. While his new business was not as lucrative, he was required to maintain alimony payments based on his previously higher income. WD #1 also wanted our relationship kept quiet because he was not ready to go public or make a commitment. After three months of these antics, I got tired and believed him.

W WD #2 was a 47-year-old actor who had been married for only four months—though this was long enough for him to lose all faith in that sacred institution. While there were no children, WD #2 had been emotionally wounded by his quick courtship (six months), marriage, and her sudden, unanticipated departure. However, his wallet was primarily unaffected because she had money. Instead, the emotional trauma prevented him from handling a relationship. He wanted to spend time with me almost every day, but made no bones that a long-term commitment was out of the question. I was smarter the second time and bowed out of this relationship after six weeks.

Even though both WDs told me about their hardships and inability to commit, I still tried to make it happen. I told myself that our connection was strong enough to break their WD state of mind. In the end, I stopped kidding myself and today value their friendships with greater understanding. Both men continue to be determinedly single.

Wounded Divorcé Strategies

I recommend strongly that you listen to these warning messages early. Do not try to fix WDs. Give them time to recover at their own pace, while you move on to other opportunities. Avoid trying to convince yourself that you alone can fix what ails them. That miracle drug has yet to be invented.

Be careful not to misinterpret their desires to be physical for an emotional connection. They are wounded and want to be cuddled. However, they cannot mentally attach to you or any other female partner.

You need to take care of yourself first. Do not get hung up in a pattern of trying to fix WDs. While women tend to be nurturers, I recommend passes on these cases. His issues are not your responsibility, and the sooner you let go, the better chance you will have to meet someone who is mentally available.

Once you make a concrete decision to part ways, decide if you value the companionship enough to continue a friendship. Evaluate whether you can emotionally and physically detach. If you are open to a friendship, always give yourself a separation period first. You will need to build your ego back to a healthy state so spend time with available men to increase your confidence. You can later resume a friendship with the WD.

Wounded Divorcé LIFE Questions

1. Can you tell me about your relationship with your ex?

2. How did you part ways with your ex?

3. Do you want to get married again and why or why not?

XXB—XX Brain

XX Brain Definition

The XX Brain (XXB) is a male primarily focused on the XX female chromosome and has sex tattooed across his forehead. His relationships are built upon sexual thoughts and physical satisfaction. He will blatantly share his needs with you. The XX Brain does not look beyond the sexual connection and may be disappointed in the long run with his partner selection. XXBs openly expose their sexual desires from the beginning. Although men in general tend to be more physically motivated than their female counterparts, the XXB is the extreme.

XX Brain Examples

Because of the abundance of XXBs, here are three examples from my Internet dating experiences:

During our first phone call, XXB # 1 made it clear that we needed to confirm a sexual attraction in person before proceeding. He was direct about his intentions, stating, "I have to be honest with you. I love sex so if we don't connect physically, then I don't see any reason to pursue a relationship." So much for foreplay. I hit the delete key immediately in this case.

My second example is another Internet candidate I met for drinks because he was not as upfront in emails or on the phone. During our visit, XXB # 2 shared a red-alert story. After dating an Internet candidate for eight months, he suddenly discovered that she was, in his words, "an airhead." This revelation came to him during a trip to Paris where he learned she was not familiar with any Impressionist painters. I had to ask myself how he managed to date someone for that long without recognizing something so obvious. The answer

$$\boxed{\textbf{X}}$$

could only be that he was an XXB blinded by sex. I never made contact with him again.

XXB # 3 was another Internet contender. During our first ten-minute phone call, XXB # 3 divulged that his divorce was necessary because he could not carry on a conversation about his work with his wife. He needed to find an intellectual partner, he said. We clicked conversationally by sharing our international telecommunications business successes.

But then we unclicked when, in the next breath, XXB # 3 said that he was returning to a bar that evening in search of a redhead he had never met before but felt attracted too. It's truly amazing what men will tell you. Shortly after the call, I sent him an email stating that I was turned off by his comments about other women, discouraged him from taking this approach again, and took a pass on his coffee invitation. I could not find my red wig, and was not interested in sex-only men.

XX Brain Strategies

The minute you meet an XXB, run like heck. These men are so physically oriented that even when they are with you, they are constantly looking around the room for other prospective bedmates. Regardless of how attractive you may be, the XXB will always have one eye on another. Unfortunately, these candidates have not evolved into well-rounded people and make horrible partners.

You are not a sex object. No one deserves to be viewed solely as a piece of meat. Don't take the XXB's priorities and comments personally. This mindset is not your problem. Don't be fooled by flattery and see through the XXB's intentions.

Be true to yourself. Run, do not walk, and do not pass go, when you encounter the first signs of XXB behavior.

XX Brain LIFE Questions

1. What is the first thing that you notice about a woman and why?

2. Can you describe the key characteristics of women in your past relationships?

3. What are the most important aspects of a relationship for you?

YE—Young Explorer

Young Explorer Definition

The Young Explorer (YE) is a male who is more than five years younger than his female partner. These candidates are comfortable with the age gap and appreciate an older woman's companionship. The YE tends to be more mature than other men his age, and can be an excellent mate. Because they tend to have faced more life challenges, the Young Explorers will most likely enjoy your company over younger females. In addition, their youth can provide spontaneity and bring more energy to your daily routine.

Young Explorer Example

My 37-year-old girlfriend recently married a Young Explorer after less than a year of dating. This YE is a 25-year-old musician and my girlfriend is an actress. The couple met after he saw one of her theater performances. The YE was immediately intrigued and wanted to meet her.

While he was open about his desire to pursue a relationship, my friend was very apprehensive about getting involved with the Young Explorer. However, his persistence eventually persuaded her to go out on a date. She had the usual older woman insecurities about whether she could compete with the looks of candidates his age.

After six months of dating, the couple was totally committed and started making wedding plans. She recognized that this YE brought out her best qualities. He encouraged her to try new hobbies and enhance her outlook. For example, she started taking piano lessons and he convinced her to try snowboarding. In addition, this YE re-engineered her cynical perspective into a more positive and healthy outlook.

Y At the end of the courtship year, she married the Young Explorer. He addressed her age-difference concerns by making her feel beautiful inside and out. The happy couple bought a house and are planning to have children in the near future.

Young Explorer Strategies

Be cautious when considering a Young Explorer as a potential candidate. Consider his life experiences as a way to gauge his maturity compatibility. Evaluate whether his behavior matches your relationship expectations.

If you decide that you want to get involved with a Young Explorer, it is important to be very confident. You should be glowing with a positive attitude and personal satisfaction. Otherwise, your insecurities will be easy to spot and ultimately drive the YE away.

In addition, you need to give the Young Explorer room to experience life within his age range. Don't get worried or jealous if the YE wants to share time with his younger friends away from you. If you exhibit anger when he wants to run off to play, these emotional outbursts will cause unnecessary strain on the relationship.

Many people make these age-gap partnerships last for years. If a Young Explorer approaches you, don't let the difference in years automatically deter you. You may be pleasantly surprised to find a life partner below your age-comfort zone.

Young Explorer LIFE Questions

1. What do you value in a relationship with an older woman?

2. What has been your past experience dating older women?

3. How do you feel about maybe being rushed to have children with an older female partner?

ZZ—Zodiac Zealot

Zodiac Zealot Definition

The Zodiac Zealot (ZZ) believes in planetary influences on relationships. ZZs look to astrologers and often psychics for guidance about partner selection, careers, and personal goals. They believe the zodiac has a major influence on their lives far beyond simply comparing astrological signs.

Zodiac Zealot Example

I went out with a 50-year-old Acupuncturist who openly shared his beliefs in astrologers and psychics. His astrological bias was based on the fact that humans are 85 percent water consisting of the same saline solution found in the ocean. This ZZ believed that humans are electromagnetic organisms greatly influenced by the planets in the same way that the moon impacts tides.

He asked for my astrological sign along with the time, date, and place of my birth. These facts were important for him to weigh before taking the relationship further. Although I find some merit in astrology, I do not give it the same weight as this ZZ. When he compared our signs, he shared that our planetary connection was a good basis for a successful relationship. His insights gave me a new perspective on dating dynamics.

Zodiac Zealot Strategies

If you meet a Zodiac Zealot, recognize the importance of his perspective and don't immediately discount his interest. Although you may not be familiar with this territory, you might learn something by keeping an

Z open mind. The ZZ is more likely to commit to a relationship if he thinks there is an astrological connection.

Consider scheduling one visit with an astrologer to understand his beliefs better. You may find the information insightful or, at the very least, entertaining. While you may discover an astrological match, keep the feedback in perspective and evaluate other characteristics of this candidate and your relationship. If the ZZ falls into other codes that can cause turbulence in a potential partnership, you probably need to part ways. However, if the stars are on your side, you might want to take a closer look before ruling out this contender.

Zodiac Zealot LIFE Questions

1. What value do you place on astrological matches?

2. Tell me about your experience with astrologers.

3. Are there zodiac signs that you steer away from dating and why?

Appendix I

Complete Your SMART Certification

SMART Certification

Are you ready to be SMART Certified? Are you ready to go, girl? With these new SMART Man Hunting dating strategies, this certification test will be easy for you. Simply answer the following multiple-choice questions, and you will receive immediate feedback on your gained SMART Man Hunting knowledge.

SMART Certification Test

1. Before I broaden my Mr. Right Search, what needs to be in place for my Confidence Face Lift?
   a. Be happy with your life
   b. Go for your Passions
   c. Build your Support Network
   d. Pamper yourself
   e. All of the above

2. What are the success keys for the Winning Hunter's Strategy?
   a. Be patient and persistent, and don't take things too personally
   b. Bounce back from rejection
   c. Ask for help
   d. Use a Give-and-Take Approach
   e. All of the above

3. What can make a MAN Hunt and a JOB Hunt successful?
   a. Boost your numbers
   b. Define your requirements
   c. Make Friends and Don't Burn Bridges
   d. Evaluate the candidates closely
   e. All of the above

4. What New Era Dating Options can help me expand my man hunt?
    a. Check out casual Chat Rooms and Singles Events
    b. Step into Internet Dating
    c. Try Quick Shot Dating or Speed Dating
    d. Use Professional Matchmakers
    e. All of the above

5. How can I be SMART and Safe when dating via the Internet?
    a. End communications with perpetual emailers
    b. Be anonymous when emailing
    c. Never give out your home phone number prior to first meetings
    d. Use valet parking at public restaurants
    e. All of the above

6. How can I create an enticing Internet Dating Profile?
    a. Write a unique and friendly tag line
    b. Post at least two current photos
    c. Write short essays versus a book
    d. Be positive and add a little humor
    e. All of the above

7. How can the SMART ABC Man Code definitions, tales and strategies help me be smarter?
    a. Learn by example
    b. Laugh at mistakes
    c. Be more selective
    d. Run like heck from the bad ones
    e. All of the above

8. Who are the ABC New Era Men good guys?
    a. Bachelor Available (BA)
    b. Curious Male/Female (CMF)
    c. Keeper of the Fire (KOF)
    d. Nourishing Nester (NN)
    e. All of the above

9. Who are the ABC New Era Men bad guys?
    a. Hello Goodbye Guy (HGG)
    b. Internet Psycho (IP)
    c. Married But Available (MBA)
    d. XX Brain (XXB)
    e. All of the above

10. Who is a Red Flag Man?
    a. Sly Schemer
    b. Macho Mind
    c. Me-First Man
    d. All of the above

11. What are some red flag observations that I should notice on dates?
    a. Is he always late for dates?
    b. Does he take cell phone calls?
    c. Are his eyes wandering around the room?
    d. Does he only talk about himself?
    e. All of the above

12. What should I try to find out on a First Date?
    a. Is there a Chemistry Connection?
    b. What do the non-verbal clues tell me?
    c. Do I want to KISS this candidate?
    d. Is he a Red Flag Man?
    e. All of the above

13. What are some good KISS questions for a first date?
    a. What do you like to do for fun?
    b. What is your favorite vacation get-away?
    c. Where did you grow up?
    d. What is your favorite ice cream flavor?
    e. All of the above

14. What are some First Date Discussion Bloopers to avoid?
    a. Leave the checkbook in the car
    b. Leave your exes in the scrapbook
    c. Do not broadcast your faults
    d. Avoid sharing too much information
    e. All of the above

15. What can you learn about a man by asking LIFE Questions pre-wedding bells to help you avoid the "D" word?
    a. Lessons Learned
    b. Introspection
    c. Flexibility
    d. Extremes
    e. All of the above

16. What should I try to discover on a second or third date?
    a. Ask for the Foundational Facts—age, family, marital history, and hobbies
    b. Quick Qualifiers—three things that each of you seek in a mate
    c. Showstoppers—things that will end a relationship's chance
    d. Is he Emotionally Ready?
    e. All of the above

17. What should my GUT tell me?
    a. Is he genuine?
    b. Does he care about my feelings?
    c. Does he have the right core characteristics?
    d. Is he trustworthy?
    e. All of the above

18. How can I ensure a lasting bond if I start getting serious with a Mr. Right candidate?
    a. Determine the ABC Man Code(s) for your male mate
    b. Analyze his flexibility using LIFE Questions
    c. Compare your personal priorities and qualities to his codes
    d. Review the Total Man, using Man Hunt Interview Practices
    e. All of the above

19. How can I complete my Final Man Analysis?
    a. Evaluate the Pros and Cons beyond the GUT
    b. Share answers to the LIFE Questions for his SMART ABC Man Code(s)
    c. Look at the dynamics of the Dating Assessment Dance
    d. Avoid rationalizing my way out of every opportunity
    e. All of the above

20. How can I identify Mr. Perfect Match?
    a. He is a Good GUT Man
    b. He has a great attitude and knows how to compromise
    c. His SMART ABC Man Codes complement versus clash with my codes
    d. He thinks you are the hottest ticket in town!
    e. All of the above

If you answered "All of the above" for every question, give yourself a standing ovation. Congratulations, you are now SMART Man Hunting Certified for New Era dating in the 21st century!

APPENDIX II

SMART ABC Man Codes Quick Guide

SMART ABC Man Codes Quick Guide

You can use this SMART ABC Man Codes Quick Guide to check off the codes for your Mr. Right candidate and identify your type(s) when you play the LIFE Match Game.

ABC	Code	Man Code Name	What codes are your MAN?	What codes are you?
A	ASF	All Sports Fanatic		
B	BA	Bachelor Available		
C	CMF	Curious Male/Female		
D	DGI	Dysfunctional Guy with Issues		
E	ESS	Executive Search Seeker		
F	FE	Fitness Extremist		
G	GWO	Guy with Offspring		
H	HGG	Hello Goodbye Guy		
I	IP	Internet Psycho		
J	JJ	Justifying Juggler		
K	KOF	Keeper of the Fire		
L	LS	Lost Soul		
M	MBA	Married But Available		
N	NN	Nourishing Nester		
O	OO	Over-Achiever Obsessor		
P	PTS	Post Traumatic Soul		
Q	QP	Questionnaire Perfectionist		
R	RR	Relentless Renter		
S	SG	Social Guru		
T	TT	Tasmanian Traveler		
U	UA	Under-estimated Ally		
V	VV	Vacillating Vortex		
W	WD	Wounded Divorcé		
X	XXB	XX Brain		
Y	YE	Young Explorer		
Z	ZZ	Zodiac Zealot		

Use the ABC codes to have fun and help you explore LIFE Match. Share this worksheet with your Man and ask him to tell you about his code(s). Avoid making assumptions and be willing to share your woman codes. He might just get a kick out of this dialogue and you can learn a lot by asking for his opinion. Let this Dating Assessment Dance step encourage communication using a fun methodology to determine compatibility. Do you want to go the distance with this guy? Does he want to go on a life journey with you?

Thank you

Many thanks to my friends and active daters, whose insights and guidance helped me become a better person and Man Hunter. Their stories and advice can also help you find long-term happiness and Mr. Right:

Abigail, Alex, Anne, Alfred, Arthur, Angela, Alan, Anna, Adam

Brigid, Betsey, Bob, Brent, Billy, Beth, Bethany, Brad, Bert, Brett

Caroline, Caroline, Cindy, Carl, Cloud, Cynthia, Chris, Cleo

Dan, Dean, Dave, Debra, David, Doug, Dena, Diana, Dines, Donna

Emily, Elizabeth, Eleanor, Ellen, Eiko, Eric

Frances, Felice, Fady, Fred, Frank, Franco

Gail, Gayle, Gennifer, Genie, Greg

Hannah, Harry, Harris, Harriett

Irene, Ian, Ira

Jane, Janet, Jim, Jeannette, Julia, Jon, John, Joan, Joe, Mojoe, Joshua, Jack, Jeff, Jan

Kate, Katie, Kristy, Ken, Karen, Kevin, Kellie

Lenore, Londa, Laura, Lori, Larry, Lizi, LeighAnn

Mary, Marshall, Marc, Maura, Morte, Mary Helen, Margo, Mara

Nancy, Nette

Ophelia

Paula, Peter, Pete, Patrick, Patti

Quentin

Riko, Roxana, Robin, Rachel, Richard, Rob, Ronda, Randi

Susie, Sue, Sandy, Stephanie, Sheila, Saeed, Stan, Scott, Sharon, Sarah

Tacy, Tim, Tarver, Tom

Vincent, Vic, Victoria, Venus, Vicki

Warren, Wallis, Will, Walker

Xana

Yolanda, Yvette

Zoe, Zack

About the Author

Liz H. Kelly is a dating coach, author and contributing writer for *MarsVenus.com*. Liz's passion for giving relationship advice led her to develop the *SMART Man Hunting* dating approach based on her twenty years of dating experience, including Internet Dating, Professional Matchmakers, and Speed Dating, along with interviews of hundreds of active daters. Following a marriage at thirty and divorce at thirty-five in her hometown of Baltimore, Maryland, Liz expanded her network of friends and has dated primarily in Washington D.C., New York, and Los Angeles. In order to bring levity to the dating scene, she started creating ABC Man Codes at parties. These codes and new dating strategies became the basis for this book. In it, she shares her energetic enthusiasm, No-Fear Attitude, sense of humor, and total commitment to helping you find what you want in the 21st century.

To create her SMART Man Hunting dating strategy, Liz drew heavily on her corporate experience in employee training, marketing communications, and sales presentation techniques to create a Winning Hunter's Toolkit for finding "the one." Liz's Man Hunting success strategies combine well-tested management techniques, real life wisdom from happily married couples, and humor to help you navigate the modern dating scene with confidence. With a MAS/Management degree from Johns Hopkins University and BA/Economics degree from the University of Maryland, Liz has been an Assistant Vice President for Training and Communications at T. Rowe Price, Corporate Training Manager for Sprint PCS, and International Training Manager for Iridium. She most recently held positions as Vice President/Director, Customer Relationship Management for several Internet startups in Los Angeles.

Liz has shared her insights on such shows as NBC's *The Other Half,* Lifetime's *Speaking of Women's Health* and National Talk Radio's *Dinner and No Movie.* Her modern dating strategies have been featured in *Glamour, MSN Money, Smart Woman* and *Honey.*

Whether you are looking for a good catch or advising single girlfriends, Liz's book provides a balanced approach for keeping your sanity, humor and heart available while seeking Mr. Right.

About the Content Editor

Childhood friend and girl next door, Susan Thompson partnered with Liz on *SMART Man Hunting* as content editor. Thompson attended the Philadelphia College of the Performing Arts and has made a career out of being a performing artist. Susan is a singer and dancer who runs with the stars. Married for more than ten years, she is a mother and step-mom. Given Susan's successful long-term relationship, girlfriends flock to her for advice.

0-595-24639-7

Power Quotes to Energize Your Life

Power Quotes to Energize Your Life

A Motivational System to Make You
More Dynamic

Ramesh Deonaraine, Ph.D.

iUniverse, Inc.
New York Lincoln Shanghai

Power Quotes to Energize Your Life
A Motivational System to Make You More Dynamic

iUniverse, Inc.

For information address:
iUniverse, Inc.
2021 Pine Lake Road, Suite 100
Lincoln, NE 68512
www.iuniverse.com

ISBN: 0-595-28855-3 (pbk)
ISBN: 0-595-65907-1 (cloth)

Printed in the United States of America

Contents

Acknowledgements

Amanda Ashcroft, Vidya Deonaraine and Felixa Koukis offered valuable suggestions and helped with the manuscript preparation. I thank them all for their kindness.

Introduction

Why This Book?

It is a common experience that people become energized when they hear or read a powerful quote. Frequently, the quote is what they remember long after they have forgotten most of the speech or article in which it was cited. For example, on a number of occasions, students and clients have told me that a striking quote I had stated to them years earlier had become a key guidepost for their lives. As I thought of how I could quickly convey the elements of the inspirational system I have used to get dramatic improvements in attainments from those I have taught/coached/advised, I came upon the idea of a set of quotes so organized that they would imbue the reader's mind with motivational principles that greatly enhance performance. I created this book so a reader could have at hand some of the most powerful thoughts ever expressed on how to live, and uniquely arranged to motivate one to become more dynamic and achieve greater success.

This book is based on the notion that a moment of inspiration is worth many hours of exhortation. We can receive many hours of advice and guidance and it may have little effect on us. The moment a teacher/coach/advisor inspires us, however, this impels us to want to take action to live more dynamically. I have therefore focused on providing many of the most powerful inspirational thoughts available, knowing that each of these, absorbed into a reader's mind, can become a generator of dynamic living.

I have sought to provide a book that can be read very quickly and yet give an enormous amount of inspiration. This is because many of the clients I advise are very busy people. Also, I do not feel a reader should have to wade through pages of dense material to get help.

Opening this book at any page, one immediately gets powerful inspiration.

Its Uniqueness

Unlike other collections of quotes, this book is not just an accumulation or assortment. The arrangement of the chapters and their sections reflects the powerful motivational system that I have used to get remarkable improvements in achievement from many students and clients. For each topic, the quotes have been selected and organized to provide a comprehensive, inspiring perspective, offering guideposts the reader can follow to achieve excellence.

For example, look at the quotes in Chapter 1. The vibrant thoughts on each topic are so arranged that they provide a focused, energizing view of life. Very quickly, they give a powerful philosophy of life—it is as if some of the finest minds have been brought together to provide the reader, in just a few minutes, with great wisdom on how to live. This same approach has been used to order the quotes in the other chapters, so that they make the reader feel better about life and want to achieve more.

The Motivational System

From years of helping many people to achieve greater success, I have concluded that those who reach high levels of performance manifest six primary qualities, which are the focus of Chapter 1 of this book:

1. Belief in the value and significance of their lives. No matter how humble their lives, they were driven by the belief that they had a unique contribution to make, that there was something special about their lives.

2. Conviction that the opportunities they had, even if not glamorous, were the bridge to a better future and that with dynamic, intelligent living they could create better opportunities.

3. Belief that they were not weak and helpless, but had the inner power to drive toward their goals. Even when there seemed no way out of a dilemma facing them, they had the feeling that their inner desire for a resolution and for success would lead to better circumstances.

4. Readiness to take efficient action. They did not dream idly of better times but were always ready to take appropriate action to better their lives.

5. Energy that came not just from good physical health but from a deep mental desire to succeed.

6. Tremendous enthusiasm for pursuing their goals. They did not merely talk about wanting success; they showed genuine ebullience for moving toward their goals.

No matter what fears, doubts, or anxieties these achievers experience, they adhere to these qualities enough to enable them to move forward resolutely and attain worthy goals. Generally, the first three qualities lead to the manifestation of the other three. However, I have encountered a number of cases in which inspiring a person to intensify her activity and be more energetic and enthusiastic helped to sharpen her inner focus and manifest more intensely the first three qualities—appetite came with eating!

As I have helped many students and clients to attain higher levels of success, I have found that many of the qualities that are frequently extolled as key ones that lead to success can never be had unless the six qualities just described are there as preconditions. We may be told to "dream great dreams," for example, but we will never be able to unless we feel that we have something unique to offer in life—the first qual-

ity. We may be told to persevere, be disciplined, be determined in order to achieve more, but we will never be able to, and will become disillusioned and give up, unless the first three qualities are present. We may be told that to be successful we must have faith. But we will never be able to have faith and manifest it in our daily lives unless these six qualities are in us. We may be told that excellent habits lead to success but our effort to acquire these habits will falter unless we have the six primary qualities to give us the drive to acquire the habits.

Inspiring words on these qualities help to stimulate their manifestation. This is why the six sections of Chapter 1 focus on these qualities. Reading the quotes in this chapter and mulling over their significance imbue the mind with correct perceptions on the role of these qualities and energize one to utilize them effectively to have greater attainments. The nine chapters following Chapter 1 provide powerful quotes that help to intensify the application of these qualities in key areas of life, ensuring optimal living.

Chapter 2 delineates attitudes and orientation that facilitate the use of the six primary qualities to achieve more. Chapter 3 presents very motivating thoughts on time management that make possible more efficient living, and Chapter 4 offers powerful thoughts on attitudes and qualities that enable "soul refinement."

Chapter 5 is particularly relevant to those engaged in management and leadership in business, organizations, government, etc. However, the insights can be readily used to manage our own lives optimally—and what greater enterprise is there to manage than that of the people and situations in our own daily lives?

Chapter 6 gives the impetus to use mental power more effectively to magnify abilities and enhance opportunities for success. Chapter 7, especially relevant to learning and education, facilitates dynamic living in these pursuits.

Chapter 8 elevates the reader's view of art, music, history, economics, reading, writing and other fields of endeavor. I have always found that when people recognize the grandeur in these pursuits, their own

lives become brighter, more meaningful. Chapter 9 is a cogent guide to getting command over difficulties, and Chapter 10 inspires the reader to create productive and loving relationships.

Chapter 11 has concluding thoughts reminding the reader of the importance of putting into practice the principles of this book and of the benefits that would be obtained from doing so.

How to Use This Book

Reading this book from beginning to end will let you get the full range of inspiration of the powerful quotes provided and will imbue your mind with the motivational system they embody. But to get the most from this book, you should view it as inspiration from a personal coach to which you should refer often—wisdom can be elusive, and in the rush and press of daily life, you can quickly lose sight of guiding principles unless you often remind yourself of them.

The section above on "The Motivational System" stated the focus of the various chapters of this book. When you need to become more focused to deal with a challenging situation, choose parts of the book to which you feel drawn and read them. This will mobilize your internal power so you can do your best.

To deepen your application of the insights of a quote, think of its relevance to your life. Picture in your mind situations in which you could have benefited from using the guidance it provides. Even a few minutes per week of this contemplation will sharply enhance the skill with which you manage your life. It is a key principle of learning that as you focus intensely on a topic, you get deeper insights on it. So as you pay keen attention to the quotes and mull over how they can be used to improve your life, you will frequently be surprised at the insights you will get.

Perhaps because I have spent so much of my life teaching, when I encounter new knowledge I always ask myself: Who could benefit from instruction on this? How would I teach this? Asking these questions

has always provided me with valuable insights. I suggest that you also ask them. You are likely to gain valuable perceptions on how the wisdom of the quotes can be used to make you more dynamic.

What You Can Get from This Book

Based on the results I have obtained from students and clients, I believe that as you absorb the inspiration of this book into your thinking, you will become more focused and purposeful. You will see more clearly the unique contributions you can make in your daily life, and even if your circumstances seem very limited, you will begin to find ways of getting better opportunities and of coping more intelligently with adversity. You will sense more power within you to give you the drive and determination to get and achieve worthy goals. All of this will make you more action-oriented, energetic and enthusiastic. You will have a more wholesome view of life and of your role in it and will have more rewarding human relationships.

It is a truism that as we change our thoughts and attitudes, our outward circumstances begin to reflect these changes. When the powerful quotes in this book become a part of your thoughts and attitudes, the motivational system they embody will make you far more dynamic. Your joy will increase and you will have grander possibilities. I have seen this happen in many lives. It is my deepest wish that it happen in yours. May all this and more come to you!

1

Your Life, Your Opportunity, Your Power

Your Life

The privilege of a lifetime is being who you are.

—Joseph Campbell

For if there is a sin against life, it consists perhaps not so much in despairing of life as in hoping for another life and in eluding the implacable grandeur of this life.

—Albert Camus

To be what we are, and to become what we are capable of becoming, is the only end of life.

—R. L. Stevenson

Do what you can, with what you have, where you are.

—Theodore Roosevelt

To do the best you can each moment is to manifest genius in living.

—Ramesh Deonaraine

Nobody makes a greater mistake than he who does nothing because he could only do a little.

—Edmund Burke

Be not afraid of life. Believe that life is worth living and your belief will create the fact.

—William James

Your vision will become clear only when you can look into your own heart. Who looks outside, dreams; who looks inside, awakes.

—Carl Jung

Seek not, my soul, the life of immortals; but enjoy to the full the resources that are within thy reach.

—Pindar

Your Opportunity

The lure of the distant and difficult is deceptive. The great opportunity is where you are.

—John Burroughs

The greatest achievement of the human spirit is to live up to one's opportunities and make the most of one's resources.

—Vauvenargues

When we do the best we can, we never know what miracle is wrought in our life, or in the life of another.

—Helen Keller

Isn't it strange
That princes and kings,
And clowns that caper
In sawdust rings,
And common people
Like you and me
Are builders for eternity?

Each is given a bag of tools,
A shapeless mass,
A book of rules;
And each must make—
Ere life is flown—
A stumbling block
Or a stepping-stone.

—R. L. Sharpe

A wise man will make more opportunities than he finds.

—Francis Bacon

When one door closes, another opens; but we often look so long and so regretfully upon the closed door that we do not see the one which has opened for us.

—Alexander Graham Bell

Know thine opportunity.

—Pittacus

Your Power

If one advances confidently in the direction of his dreams, and endeavors to live the life which he has imagined, he will meet with a success unexpected in common hours.

—Henry David Thoreau

Deep within man dwell those slumbering powers; powers that would astonish him, that he never dreamed of possessing; forces that would revolutionize his life if aroused and put into action.

—O. S. Marsden

Most people…make use of a very small portion…of their possible consciousness…much like a man who, out of his whole bodily organism, should get into the habit of using and moving only his little finger. Great emergencies and crises show us how much greater our vital resources are than we had supposed.

—William James

Concerning all acts of initiative and creation, there is one elementary truth—the moment one definitely commits oneself, then Providence moves, too.

—Goethe

Nothing splendid has ever been achieved except by those who dared believe that something inside of them was superior to circumstance.

—Bruce Barton

I've continued to recognize the power individuals have to change virtually anything and everything in their lives in an instant. I've learned that the resources we need to turn our dreams into reality are within us, merely waiting for the day when we decide to wake up and claim our birthright.

—Anthony Robbins

Action

In the arena of human life the honors and rewards fall to those who show their good qualities in action.

—Aristotle

The quality of a life is determined by its activities.

—Aristotle

Determine never to be idle.... It is wonderful how much may be done if we are always doing.

—Thomas Jefferson

The common conception is that motivation leads to action, but the reverse is true—action precedes motivation. You have to "prime the pump" and get the juice flowing, which motivates you to work on your goals. Getting momentum going is the most difficult part of the job, and often taking the first step is enough to prompt you to make the best of your day.

—Robert Mckain

Action always generates inspiration....

—Frank Tibolt

...inaction saps the vigors of the mind.

—Leonardo da Vinci

I must lose myself in action lest I wither in despair.

—Tennyson

Energy

There is no genius in life like the genius of energy and activity.

—Donald Mitchell

Energy is eternal delight.

—William Blake

The longer I live the more I am convinced that neither age nor circumstance need deprive us of energy and vitality.

—Norman Vincent Peale

Energy is equal to desire and purpose.

—Sheryl Adams

Vitality shows in not only the ability to persist but the ability to start over.

—F. Scott Fitzgerald

Enthusiasm

Zest is the secret of all beauty. There is no beauty that is attractive without zest.

—Christian Dior

Exuberance is beauty.

—William Blake

Enthusiasm is the greatest asset in the world. It beats money, power and influence.

—Henry Chester

If you can give your son or daughter only one gift, let it be enthusiasm.

—Bruce Barton

Enthusiasm…the sustaining power of all great action.

—Samuel Smiles

…make a high and holy resolve that you will double the amount of enthusiasm that you have been putting into your work and into your life. If you carry out that resolve, you will probably also double…your happiness.

—Dale Carnegie

To become enthusiastic—act enthusiastic.

—Frank Bettger

Nothing great or new can be done without enthusiasm.

—Harvey Cushing

Man never rises to great truths without enthusiasm.

—Vauvenargues

2

Toward Optimum Performance

Dreams

The mightiest works have been accomplished by men who have somehow kept their ability to dream great dreams.

—Walter Russell Bowie

Reach high, for stars lie hidden in your soul. Dream deep, for every dream precedes a goal.

—Pamela Vaull Starr

Nothing happens unless first a dream.

—Carl Sandburg

There is nothing like a dream to create the future.

—Victor Hugo

You are what your deep, driving desire is.
As your desire is, so is your will.
As your will is, so is your deed.
As your deed is, so is your destiny.

—Upanishad

Whatever you vividly imagine, ardently desire, sincerely believe, and enthusiastically act upon, must inevitably come to pass.

—Paul Meyer

Slight not what's near through aiming at what's far.

—Euripides

Aim not too high nor too low.

—Anonymous

Dreams are renewable. No matter what our age or condition, there are still untapped possibilities within us and new beauty waiting to be born.

—Dale Turner

Achievement

If we did the things we are capable of doing, we would literally astound ourselves.

—Thomas Edison

I know of no more encouraging fact than the unquestionable ability of man to elevate his life by conscious endeavor.

—Henry David Thoreau

It has long since come to my attention that people of accomplishment rarely sat back and let things happen to them. They went out and happened to things.

—Elinor Smith

The success of those less able than you is evidence abundant of what you can have if you start and continue working to do your best.

—Ramesh Deonaraine

Nobody can contribute to the best of humanity who does not make the best of himself.

—Johann Gottfried Herder

There is no one else who can fill your role in the same way, so it is a good idea to perform it as well as possible.

—Humphry Osmond

Achievement is a habit—cultivate it.

—Harry Mills

Excellence

The excellent is new forever.

—Emerson

What is our praise or pride
But to imagine excellence and try to make it?

—Richard Wilbur

If something is exceptionally well done, it has embedded in its very existence the aim of lifting the common denominator rather than catering to it.

—Edward Fischer

If we want to make something really superb on this planet, there is nothing whatever that can stop us.

—Shepherd Mead

The price of excellence is discipline.

—William Ward

Great things are not done by impulse, but by a series of small things brought together.

—Vincent van Gogh

The will to win, the desire to succeed, the urge to reach your full potential…these are the keys that will unlock the door to personal excellence.

—Eddie Robinson

It takes a long time to bring excellence to maturity.

—Publilius Syrus

Excellence is the gradual result of always striving to do better.

—Pat Riley

Excellence is doing ordinary things extraordinarily well.

—John W. Gardner

High achievement always takes place in the framework of high expectation.

—Jack Kinder

Work

Do, and the urge to do will come.

—Anonymous

Just as appetite comes by eating, so work brings inspiration, if inspiration is not discernible at the beginning.

—Igor Stravinsky

I am a great believer in luck, and I find the harder I work, the more I have of it.

—Thomas Jefferson

The best preparation for good work tomorrow is to do good work today.

—Elbert Hubbard

Do your work with your whole heart and you will succeed—there is so little competition!

—Elbert Hubbard

For every disciplined effort there is a multiple reward.

—Jim Rohn

Make your job important and it will return the favor.

—Arnold Glasgow

...many things which cannot be overcome when they are together, yield themselves up when taken little by little.

—Plutarch

Little strokes fell great oaks.

—English proverb

Work is and always has been my salvation and I thank the Lord for it.

—Louisa May Alcott

Hard Work

The heights by great men reached and kept
Were not attained by sudden flight,

But they, while their companions slept,
Were toiling upward in the night.

—Longfellow

I do not know of anyone who has got to the top without hard work.

—Margaret Thatcher

Hard work has made it easy. That is my secret. That is why I win.

—Nadia Comaneci

When I was a young man I observed that nine out of ten things I did were failures. I didn't want to be a failure, so I did ten times more work.

—George Bernard Shaw

Genius is one percent inspiration and ninety nine percent perspiration.

—Thomas Edison

You can have unbelievable intelligence, you can have connections, you can have opportunities fall out of the sky. But in the end, hard work is the true, enduring characteristic of successful people.

—Marsha Evans

Initiative

Whatever you can do, or dream you can, begin it. Boldness has genius, power, and magic in it.

—Goethe

Genius is initiative on fire.

—Holbrook Jackson

Winning starts with beginning.

—Anonymous

The first two letters of the word goal spell go.

—Anonymous

All glory comes from daring to begin.

—Anonymous

The secret of getting ahead is getting started. The secret of getting started is breaking your complex, overwhelming tasks into small, manageable tasks, and then starting on the first one.

—Mark Twain

Perhaps the most valuable result of all education is the ability to make yourself do the thing you have to do, when it ought to be done, whether you like it or not; it is the first lesson that ought to be learned, and however early a man's training begins, it is probably the last lesson that he learns thoroughly.

—Thomas Huxley

Make hay while the sun shines.

—English proverb

Knowing is not enough; we must apply; willing is not enough; we must do.

—Goethe

Perseverance, Discipline

Nothing can take the place of persistence. Talent will not; nothing is more common than unsuccessful men with talent. Genius will not; the world is full of educated derelicts. Persistence and determination alone are omnipotent. The slogan "press on" has solved and always will solve the problems of the human race.

—Calvin Coolidge

Perseverance is a great element of success. If you only knock long enough and loud enough at the gate, you are sure to wake up somebody.

—Longfellow

The wayside of business is full of brilliant men who started out with a spurt, and lacked the stamina to finish. Their places were taken by patient and unshowy plodders who never knew when to quit.

—J.R. Todd

The will to persevere is often the difference between failure and success.

—David Sarnoff

Perseverance is not a long race; it is many short races one after another.

—Walter Elliott

No life ever grows until it is focused, dedicated, disciplined.

—Harry Emerson Fosdick

The person who makes a success of living is the one who sees his goal steadily and aims for it unswervingly. That is dedication.

—Cecil B. De Mille

What we do upon some great occasion will probably depend on what we already are. What we are will be the result of previous years of self-discipline.

—Henry Parry Liddon

Never despair, but if you do, work on in despair.

—Edmund Burke

Determination

There is no chance, no destiny, no fate,
Can circumvent or hinder or control
The firm resolve of a determined soul.

—Ella Wheeler Wilcox

Nothing great will ever be achieved without great men, and men are great only if they are determined to be so.

—Charles de Gaulle

The longer I live, the more certain I am that the great difference between the great and the insignificant, is energy—invincible determination....

—Sir Thomas Fowell Buxton

What this power is I cannot say; all I know is that it exists and it becomes available only when a man is in that state of mind

in which he knows exactly what he wants and is fully determined not to quit until he finds it.

—Alexander Graham Bell

Faith

Getting ahead in a difficult profession requires avid faith in
yourself. You must be able to sustain yourself against stagger-
ing blows. There is no code of conduct to help beginners. That
is why some people with mediocre talent, but with great inner
drive, go much further than people with vastly superior talent.

—Sophia Loren

It is only by risking our persons from one hour to another that
we live at all. And often enough our faith beforehand in an
uncertified result is the only thing that makes the result come
true.

—William James

Faith is the substance of things hoped for, the evidence of
things not seen.

—Bible

Faith is to believe what we do not see, and the reward of this
faith is to see what we believe.

—St. Augustine

Faith—is the Pierless Bridge
Supporting what We see
Unto the Scene that We do not.

—Emily Dickinson

Faith is an excitement and an enthusiasm: it is a condition of intellectual magnificence to which we must cling as to a treasure, and not squander....

—George Sand

Maturity

The immature mind hops from one thing to another; the mature mind seeks to follow through.

—Harry Overstreet

...the sign of maturity is accepting deferred gratification.

—Peggy Cahn

The process of maturing is an art to be learned, an effort to be sustained.

—Marya Mannes

We have not passed the subtle line between childhood and adulthood until we move from the passive voice to the active voice—that is, until we have stopped saying "It got lost," and say, "I lost it."

—Sydney J. Harris

Maturity is the birth of a sense of fellowship with other human beings as we take our place among them.

—Virginia Woolf

Maturity is the ability to give love and receive it joyously and without guilt.

—Leo Baeck

The turning point in the process of growing up is when you discover the core of strength within you that survives all hurt.

—Max Lerner

Maturity is the capacity to endure uncertainty.

—John Finley

Courage, Confidence

Every man has his own courage, and is betrayed because he seeks in himself the courage of other persons.

—Emerson

When you get into a tight place and everything goes against you, till it seems as though you could not hold on a minute longer, never give up then, for that is just the place and the time the tide will turn.

—Harriet Beecher Stowe

Courage is resistance to fear, mastery of fear, not absence of fear.

—Mark Twain

Confidence is that feeling by which the mind embarks on great and honorable courses with a sure hope and trust in itself.

—Cicero

Confidence doesn't come out of nowhere. It's a result of something…hours and days and weeks and years of constant work and dedication.

—Roger Staubach

Confidence and courage come through preparation and practice.

—Anonymous

Patience

No road is too long to the man who advances deliberately and without undue haste; and no honors are too distant for the man who prepares himself for them with patience.

—Bruyere

Patience and diligence, like faith, remove mountains.

—William Penn

...the patient conquest of difficulties which rise in the regular and legitimate channels of business and enterprise is not only essential in securing the success which you seek but it is essential to that preparation of your mind, requisite for the enjoyment of your successes, and for retaining them when gained.

—Josiah Gilbert Holland

You can't push a wave onto the shore any faster than the ocean brings it in.

—Susan Strasberg

Patience is a bitter plant but is has a sweet fruit.

—German proverb

Whoever has no patience has no wisdom.

—Sa'di

Patience in one moment of anger will save you a thousand days of sorrow.

—Anonymous

Hope

Do not grope
Among the shadows of old sins, but let
thine own soul's light shine on the path of
hope.

—Ella Wheeler Wilcox

Hope, like a gleaming taper's light,
Adorns and cheers our way;
And still, as darker grows the night,
Emits a brighter ray.

—Oliver Goldsmith

One of the best safeguards of our hopes…is to be able to mark
off the areas of hopelessness and to acknowledge them, to face
them directly, not with despair but with the creative intent of
keeping them from polluting all the areas of possibility.

—William F. Lynch

Hope must always be tempered with a realistic assessment of
our prospects. We must ask: Does evidence from human life
suggest that what I hope for is possible? Does evidence from
my life suggest that what I hope for is attainable?

—Ramesh Deonaraine

Habits

We are what we repeatedly do. Excellence, then, is not an act,
but a habit.

—Aristotle

Achievement is a habit—cultivate it.

—Harry Mills

To learn new habits is everything, for it is to reach the substance of life. Life is but a tissue of habits.

—Henri Amiel

What it lies in our power to do, it lies in our power not to do.

—Aristotle

We must first make our habits, and then our habits make us.

—John Dryden

Habit is either the best of servants or the worst of masters.

—Nathaniel Emmons

What a curious phenomenon it is that you can get people to die for the liberty of the world who will not make the little sacrifice that is needed to free themselves from their own individual bondage.

—Bruce Barton

Attitudes

The greatest discovery of my generation is that a human being can alter his life by altering his attitudes of mind.

—William James

Our attitudes control our lives; attitudes are a secret power working twenty-four hours a day, for good or bad. It is of paramount importance that we know how to harness and control this great force.

—Charles Simmons

Adopting the right attitude can convert a negative stress into a positive one.

—Hans Selye

There is little difference in people, but that little difference makes a big difference. That little difference is attitude. The big difference is whether it is positive or negative.

—W. Clement Stone

The mind is a dangerous weapon, even to its possessor, if he knows not discreetly how to use it.

—Montaigne

The mind is its own place, and in itself
Can make a heaven of hell, or a hell of heaven.

—Milton

Self-reliance

The wise don't expect to find life worth living. They make it that way.

—Anonymous

The future depends on many things, but mostly on you.

—Frank Tyger

The best things in life must come by effort from within, not by gifts from outside.

—Fred Corson

He who would be well taken care of must take care of himself.

—William Graham Sumner

I believe you have to make your own opportunity. You really have to get going. Get out! Find them!

—Diana Ross

Faced with crisis, the man of character falls back on himself.

—Charles de Gaulle

3

Today! Today! Today!

Today

Look to this day!
For it is life, the very life of life.
In its brief course
Lie all the verities and realities of your existence:
The bliss of growth,
The glory of action,
The splendor of achievement.
For yesterday is but a dream,
And tomorrow is only a vision:
But today well-lived makes
Every yesterday a dream of happiness,
And every tomorrow a vision of hope.

—Kalidasa

Every day is a fresh beginning,
Every morn the world is made new.

—Susan Coolidge

Each day the world is born anew
For him who takes it rightly.

—James Russell Lowell

Yesterday is a cancelled check.
Tomorrow is a promissory note.
Today is ready cash. Use it!

—Anonymous

It is only possible to live happily ever after on a day-to-day basis.

—Margaret Bonnano

The best preparation for good work tomorrow is to do good work today.

—Elbert Hubbard

We forget that every good that is worth possessing must be paid for in strokes of daily effort. We postpone and postpone, until those smiling possibilities are dead.

—William James

The day is always his who works in it with serenity and great aims.

—Emerson

Now, This Moment

I always say to myself, what is the most important thing we can think about at this extraordinary moment.

—R. Buckminster Fuller

To do the best you can each moment is to manifest genius in living.

—Ramesh Deonaraine

Our main business is not to see what lies dimly at a distance, but to do what lies clearly at hand.

—Thomas Carlyle

The present time has one advantage over every other—it is our own.

—Charles Colton

The present is a gift. Accept it, use it well.

—Anonymous

Love the moment and the energy of that moment will spread beyond all boundaries.

—Corita Kent

Life is a succession of moments.
To live each one is to succeed.

—Corita Kent

Past and Future

Waste no tears
Upon the blotted record of lost years,
But turn the leaf and smile, oh, smile, to see
The fair white pages that remain for thee.

—Ella Wheeler Wilcox

Look not mournfully into the Past. It comes not back again. Wisely improve the Present. It is thine. Go forth to meet the shadowy Future, without fear....

—Longfellow

The future belongs to those who believe in the beauty of their dreams.

—Eleanor Roosevelt

As for the future, your task is not to foresee, but to enable it.

—Saint-Exupery

The future does not get better by hope—it gets better by plan.

—Jim Rohn

The best way to predict your future is to create it.

—Stephen Covey

Real generosity toward the future lies in giving all to the present.

—Albert Camus

If what you are doing now is inconsistent with your future goals, how will you get to that future?

—Ramesh Deonaraine

All our yesterdays are summarized in our now, and all the tomorrows are ours to shape.

—Hal Borland

A New Beginning, One Step at a Time

Winning starts with beginning.

—Anonymous

It is never too late—in fiction or in life—to revise.

—Nancy Thayer

Life never presents us with anything which may not be looked upon as a fresh starting point, no less than as a termination.

—Andre Gide

Though no one can go back and make a brand new start, anyone can start from now and make a brand new ending.

—Carl Bard

Even the tallest towers begin from the ground.

—Chinese proverb

A journey of a thousand miles begins with a single step.

—Lao Tse

If you only keep adding little by little, it will become a big heap.

—Hesiod

He who would learn to fly one day must first learn to stand and walk and run and climb and dance; one cannot fly into flying.

—Friedrich Nietzche

Perseverance is not a long race; it is many short races one after another.

—Walter Elliott

Time

Every morning you are handed 24 golden hours. They are one of the few things in this world that you get free of charge. If you had all the money in the world, you couldn't buy an extra hour. What will you do with this priceless treasure?

—Anonymous

To get all there is out of living, we must employ our time wisely, never being in too much of a hurry to stop and sip life, but never losing our sense of the enormous value of a minute.

—Robert Updegraff

You will never find the time for anything. If you want time, you must make it.

—Charles Buston

To every thing there is a season, and a time to every purpose under the heaven.

—Bible

The time to repair the roof is when the sun is shining.

—John F. Kennedy

Anything that is wasted effort represents wasted time. The best management of our time thus becomes linked inseparably with the best utilization of our efforts.

—Ted W. Engstrom

Things which matter most must never be at the expense of things which matter least.

—Goethe

I would willingly stand at street corners, hat in hand, begging passers-by to drop their unused minutes into it.

—Bernard Berenson

4

Soul Refinement

Kindness

Three things in life are important. The first is to be kind. The second is to be kind. And the third is to be kind.

—Henry James

There is no exercise better for the heart than reaching down and lifting people up.

—John Andrew Holmer

Kindness can become its own motive. We are made kind by being kind.

—Eric Hoffer

There is no beautifier of complexion, or form, or behavior, like the wish to scatter joy and not pain around us.

—Emerson

Human kindness has never weakened the stamina or softened the fiber of a free people. A nation does not have to be cruel to be tough.

—Franklin D. Roosevelt

Kind words can be short and easy to speak, but their echoes are truly endless.

—Mother Teresa

Gratitude

A thankful spirit is like sunshine upon the fields.

—Anonymous

Gratitude is the fairest blossom which springs from the soul.

—Ballou

Gratitude unlocks the fullness of life. It turns what we have into enough, and more. It turns denial into acceptance, chaos to order, confusion to clarity. It can turn a meal into a feast, a house into a home, a stranger into a friend. Gratitude makes sense of our past, brings peace for today and creates a vision for tomorrow.

—Melody Beattie

Gratefulness is the acknowledgement of the true sources of our strengths and attainments.

—Ramesh Deonaraine

The person who has stopped being thankful has fallen asleep in life.

—R. L. Stevenson

Gratitude is the most exquisite form of courtesy.

—Jacques Maritain

Gratitude is the memory of the heart.

—Massieu

If I have seen further, it is by standing on the shoulders of giants.

—Sir Isaac Newton

Humility

To be humble to superiors is duty, to equals courtesy, to inferiors nobleness.

—Benjamin Franklin

We come nearest to the great when we are great in humility.

—Rabindranath Tagore

A mango tree loaded with fruit bends to the ground; the one without fruit stands tall.

—Indian proverb

Anyone can be polite to a king, but it takes a civilized person to be polite to a beggar.

—Anonymous

Listening, Communication

Listening is a magnetic and strange thing, a creative force. The friends who listen to us are the ones we move toward, and we want to sit in their radius. When we are listened to, it creates us, makes us unfold and expand.

—Karl Menninger

One friend, one person who is truly understanding, who takes the trouble to listen to us as we consider our problems, can change our whole outlook on the world.

—Elton Mayo

If I can listen to what he tells me, if I can understand how it seems to him, if I can sense the emotional flavor which it has

for him, then I will be releasing potent forces of change within him.

—Carl Rogers

The most difficult thing in the world is to say thinkingly what everybody says without thinking.

—Alain

What is conceived well is expressed clearly,
And the words to say it with arrive with ease.

—Nicolas Boileau

Only an incompetent mind is content to express itself incompetently.

—J. M. Barker

Cheerfulness, Calmness, Serenity

The path to cheerfulness is to sit cheerfully and to act and speak as if cheerfulness were already there.

—William James

Developing a cheerful disposition can permit an atmosphere wherein one's spirit can be nurtured and encouraged to blossom and bear fruit. Being pessimistic and negative about our experiences will not enhance the quality of our lives. A determination to be of good cheer can help us and those around us to enjoy life more fully.

—Barbara Winder

Cheerfulness keeps up a kind of daylight in the mind and fills it with a steady and perpetual serenity.

—Joseph Addison

Quiet minds cannot be perplexed or frightened, but go on...at their own private pace, like a clock during a thunderstorm.

—R. L. Stevenson

The day is always his who works in it with serenity and great aims.

—Emerson

He is a first-rate collector who can, upon all occasions, collect his wits.

—Dennison Prentice

The swallows of sorrow may fly overhead, but don't let them nest in your hair.

—Chinese proverb

Charm, Tact

Charm is having such a glow within you that you cast a becoming light on others.

—Anonymous

Tact is the knack of making a point without making an enemy.

—Howard Newton

Tact is the intelligence of the heart.

—Anonymous

Silence is not always tact, and it is tact that is golden, not silence.

—Samuel Butler

Remember not only to say the right thing in the right place, but far more difficult still, to leave unsaid the wrong thing at the tempting moment.

—Benjamin Franklin

A smile at the right time is worth a thousand words.

—Anonymous

Some people mistake weakness for tact. If they are silent when they ought to speak and so feign an agreement they do not feel, they call it being tactful. Cowardice would be a better name.

—Sir Frank Medlicott

Clarity, Simplicity

There is a poignancy in all things clear....

—Richard Wilbur

The trouble with so many of us is that we underestimate the power of simplicity. We have a tendency it seems to over complicate our lives and forget what's important and what's not. We tend to mistake movement for achievement. We tend to focus on activities instead of results. And as the pace of life continues to race along in the outside world, we forget that we have the power to control our lives regardless of what's going on outside.

—Richard Stuberg

Simplicity is the most difficult thing to secure in this world; it is the last limit of experience and the last effort of genius.

—George Sand

Making the simple complicated is commonplace; making the complicated simple, awesomely simple, that's creativity.

—Charles Mingus

Everything should be made as simple as possible....

—Albert Einstein

For me the greatest beauty always lay in the greatest clarity.

—Gotthold Ephraim Lessing

It is proof of high culture to be able to say the greatest things in the simplest ways.

—Emerson

Luck

Luck is a matter of preparation meeting opportunity.

—Oprah Winfrey

Care and diligence bring luck.

—Thomas Fuller

I am a great believer in luck, and I find the harder I work, the more I have of it.

—Thomas Jefferson

Fortune favors those who are prepared.

—Anonymous

Diligence is the mother of good luck, and God gives all things to industry.

—Benjamin Franklin

Luck is being ready for the chance.

—J. Frank Dobie

In the field of observation, chance favors the prepared mind.

—Louis Pasteur

Go and wake up your luck.

—Persian proverb

Let the fool prate of luck. The fortunate
Is he whose earnest purpose never swerves,
Whose slightest action or inaction serves
The one great aim....

—Ella Wheeler Wilcox

Opportunities are usually disguised as hard work, so most people don't recognize them.

—Ann Landers

Youthfulness

I am perhaps the oldest musician in the world. I am an old man but in many senses a very young man. And this is what I want you to be, young, young all your life, and to say things to the world that are true.

—Pablo Casals, age 95, at a concert

The longer I live the more I am convinced that neither age nor circumstance need to deprive us of energy and vitality.

—Norman Vincent Peale

Zest for living makes the spirit grow younger.

—Ramesh Deonaraine

Time—our youth—it never really goes, does it? It is all held in our minds.

—Helen Hoover Santmyer

When I was young I was amazed at Plutarch's statement that the elder Cato began at the age of eighty to learn Greek. I am amazed no longer. Old age is ready to undertake tasks that youth shirked because they would take too long.

—Somerset Maugham

What grows never grows old.

—Noah benShea

The belief that youth is the happiest time of life is founded upon a fallacy. The happiest person is the person who thinks the most interesting thoughts, and we grow happier as we grow older.

—William Lyon Phelps

Age gives us the great opportunity to add to the energy and ebullience of youth, power, purpose, wisdom, and achievement, without which the dreams of youth are only gaudy bubbles.

—Ramesh Deonaraine

Youthfulness is a measure of the dynamism with which we live, not a measure of our age.

—Ramesh Deonaraine

Character

We sow a thought and reap an act,
We sow an act and reap a habit,

We sow a habit and reap a character,
We sow a character and reap a destiny.

—Thackeray

Character is simply habit long enough continued.

—Plutarch

To guarantee your character becomes the best, do the best you can and help others live to their best.

—Ramesh Deonaraine

A person's character is the arbiter of his fortune.

—Publilius Syrus

A man's character is his guardian divinity.

—Heraclitus

Character is the architecture of the soul.

—Ramesh Deonaraine

No man can climb out beyond the limitations of his own character.

—John Morley

Happiness

Be happy. It is a way of being wise.

—Colette

The mind in its own place, and in itself
Can make a heaven of hell, or hell of heaven.

—Milton

Like swimming, riding, writing or playing golf, happiness can be learned.

—Boris Sokoloff

Learn how to feel joy.

—Seneca

The greater part of our happiness or misery depends on our dispositions, and not our circumstances.

—Martha Washington

Happiness is a perfume you cannot pour on others without getting a few drops on yourself.

—Anonymous

The grand essentials to happiness in this life are something to do; something to love; and something to hope for.

—Joseph Addison

The happiest people are those who think the most interesting thoughts. Those who decide to use leisure as a means of mental development, who love good music, good books, good pictures, good company, good conversation, are the happiest people in the world. And they are not only happy in themselves, they are the cause of happiness in others.

—William Lyon Phelps

The secret of happiness is this: let your interests be as wide as possible, and let your reactions to the things and persons that interest you be as far as possible friendly rather hostile.

—Bertrand Russell

Have a variety of interests…. These interests relax the mind and lessen tension on the nervous system. People with many interests live not only longest, but happiest.

—George Matthew Allen

This is the true joy—the being used for a purpose recognized as a mighty one.

—George Bernard Shaw

Happiness is often the result of being too busy to be miserable.

—Anonymous

Beauty

We are living in a world of beauty but how few of us open our eyes to see it! What a different place this would be if our senses were trained to see and hear! We are the heirs of wonderful treasures from the past: treasures of literature and of the arts. They are ours for the asking—all our own to enjoy, if only we desire them enough.

—Lorado Taft

Though we travel the world over to find the beautiful, we must carry it with us or we find it not.

—Emerson

Exuberance is beauty.

—William Blake

Zest is the secret of all beauty. There is no beauty that is attractive without zest.

—Christian Dior

A thing of beauty is a joy for ever:
Its loveliness increases; it will never
Pass into nothingness.

—John Keats

5

Leadership

Leadership

Leaders aren't born, they are made. And they are made just like anything else, through hard work. And that's the price we'll have to pay to achieve that goal, or any goal.

—Vince Lombardi

...the most successful leader of all is the one who sees another picture not yet actualized. He sees the things which belong in his present picture but which are not yet there....

—Mary Parker Follett

A leader is someone who helps improve the lives of other people or improve the systems they live under.

—Sam Ervin

The true leader makes his followers twice the men they were before.

—Stephen Neill

The leader seeks to communicate his vision to his followers. He captures their attention with his optimistic intuition of possible solutions to their needs. He influences them by the

dynamism of his faith. He demonstrates confidence that the challenge can be met, the need resolved, the crisis overcome.

—John Haggai

The leader must know, must know that he knows, and must be able to make it abundantly clear to those about him that he knows.

—Clarence B. Randall

The chief executive who knows his strengths and weaknesses as a leader is likely to be far more effective than the one who remains blind to them. He also is on the road to humility—that priceless attitude of openness to life that can help a manager absorb mistakes, failures, or personal shortcomings.

—John Adair

No man will make a great leader who wants to do it all himself, or to get all the credit for doing it.

—Andrew Carnegie

In really good companies, you have to lead. You have to come up with big ideas and express them forcefully. I have always been encouraged—or sometimes forced—to confront the very natural fear of being wrong. I was constantly pushed to find out what I really thought and then to speak up. Over time, I came to see that waiting to discover which way the wind was blowing is an excellent way to learn how to be a follower.

—Roger Enrico

Leadership is the wise use of power. Power is the capacity to translate intention into reality and sustain it.

—Warren Bennis

No matter what is your occupation, you manifest leadership if you seek the best from yourself and awaken others to do the best they can.

—Ramesh Deonaraine

A great leader does not just help people to get what they want. He guides them to want what is truly best and inspires them to achieve.

—Ramesh Deonaraine

To lead **yourself** to do what is truly best is perhaps the greatest leadership task you will face in this life.

—Ramesh Deonaraine

He who has never learned to obey cannot be a good commander.

—Aristotle

What you cannot enforce,
Do not command.

—Sophocles

Management works in the system. Leadership works on the system.

—Stephen Covey

Management

Man is the principal syllable in management.

—C. T. McKenzie

The foremost distinguishing feature of effective managers seems to be their ability to recognize talent and to surround themselves with able colleagues.

—Norman Augustine

I would rather have a first-class manager running a second-rate business than a second-rate manager running a first-rate business.

—John W. Teets

Each successful manager soon discovers that problem analysis is crucial to effective leadership.

—Jard Deville

Executives who get there and stay suggest solutions when they present the problems.

—Malcolm S. Forbes

Effective managers must not just see vividly the business as it is but must also have a clear vision of what the business is to become.

—Ramesh Deonaraine

Great managers are readily able to imbue those they manage with the spirit to move energetically toward the desired future.

—Ramesh Deonaraine

Discernment, the exercise of keen judgment so essential for excellence in management, is a skill that should be carefully nurtured, and to which inadequate attention is paid in much management training. To hone the ability to act judiciously takes great discipline, deep thought, and the intense desire to learn from mistakes.

—Ramesh Deonaraine

Team-building

Of all the things I've done, the most vital is coordinating the talents of those who work for us and pointing them towards a certain goal.

—Walt Disney

Teamwork is the ability to work together toward a common vision, the ability to direct individual accomplishments toward organizational objectives. It is the fuel that allows common people to attain uncommon results.

—Anonymous

Clearly no group can as an entity create ideas. Only individuals can do this. A group of individuals may, however, stimulate one another in the creation of ideas.

—Estill I. Green

Talent wins games, but teamwork wins championships.

—Michael Jordan

Getting individuals to work with you adds to your collective power. Molding these individuals into a team multiplies your power.

—Ramesh Deonaraine

Listening, Communication

See the quotes in Chapter 4 under "Listening, Communication."

Leadership and communication are inseparable.

—Claude Taylor

Skill in the art of communication is crucial to a leader's success. He can accomplish nothing unless he can communicate effectively.

—Norman Allen

Feedback, Coaching

Feedback is the breakfast of champions.

—Kenneth Blanchard
& Spencer Johnson

In a meritocracy, nothing is more important [than feedback].

—Jack Welch

I never criticize a player until they are first convinced of my unconditional confidence in their abilities.

—John Robinson

A good coach will make his players see what they can be rather than what they are.

—Ara Parasheghian

A good hitting instructor is able to mold his teaching to the individual. If a guy stands on his head, you perfect that.

—Bill Robinson

Coaches have to watch for what they don't want to see and listen to what they don't want to hear.

—John Madden

Remember not only to say the right thing in the right place, but far more difficult still, to leave unsaid the wrong thing at the tempting moment.

—Benjamin Franklin

A great coach is very able at teaching how to handle failure intelligently. Indeed, possession of this one ability is probably what makes a coach great.

—Ramesh Deonaraine

Judgment, Decisions

See the quotes in Chapter 6 under "Judgment, Decisions."

Rule # 1—"Use your good judgment in all situations." There will be no additional rules.

—Nordstrom Employee Manual

Discernment, the exercise of keen judgment so essential for excellence in management, is a skill that should be carefully nurtured, and to which inadequate attention is paid in much management training. To hone the ability to act judiciously takes great discipline, deep thought, and the intense desire to learn from mistakes.

—Ramesh Deonaraine

Problem Solving

Can it be that man is essentially a being who loves to conquer difficulties, a creature whose function is to solve problems?

—Gorham Munson

Each successful manager soon discovers that problem analysis is crucial to effective leadership.

—Jard Deville

Executives who get there and stay suggest solutions when they present the problems.

—Malcolm S. Forbes

Peak performers concentrate on solving problems rather than placing blame for them.

—Charles Garfield

A problem is a chance for you to do your best.

—Duke Ellington

View thinking as a strategy. Thinking is the best way to resolve difficulties. Maintain faith in your ability to think your way out of your problems. Recognize the difference between worrying and thinking. The former is repeated, needless problem analysis while the latter is solution generation.

—Timothy Firnstahl

There is a technique, a knack for thinking, just as there is for doing other things. [Your thoughts] are a machine you can learn to operate.

—Alfred North Whitehead

A problem well stated is half solved.

—John Dewey

Passion, Motivation, Morale

Without passion man is a mere latent force and possibility, like the flint which awaits the shock of the iron before it can give forth its spark.

—Henri Amiel

Three people were at work on a construction site. All were doing the same job, but when each was asked what his job was, the answers varied. "Breaking rocks," the first replied. "Earning my living," the second said. "Helping to build a cathedral," said the third.

—Peter Schultz

No business or organization can become great unless its leaders are very passionate about its operation and goals. No life can become great without a deep passion for achievement.

—Ramesh Deonaraine

Before you can inspire with emotion, you must be swamped with it yourself.
Before you can move their tears, your own must flow. To convince them, you must yourself believe.

—Winston Churchill

Passion is the trigger of success.

—Anonymous

Passion is in all great searches and is necessary to all creative endeavors.

—Eugene W. Smith

People are failures, not because they are stupid, but because they are not sufficiently impassioned.

—Burt Struthers

Striving for excellence motivates you; striving for perfection is demoralizing.

—Harriet Braiker

Motivation will almost always beat mere talent.

—Norman Augustine

Motivation is like food for the brain. You cannot get enough in one sitting. It needs continual and regular top ups.

—Peter Davies

Motivation is what gets you started. Habit is what keeps you going.

—Jim Ryun

[Morale] is steadfastness and courage and hope. It is confidence and zeal and loyalty. It is élan, esprit de corps and determination.

—George Marshall

The best morale exists when you never hear the word mentioned. When you hear a lot of talk about it, it's usually lousy.

—Dwight Eisenhower

A business, organization, department or life without high morale is like a great machine on stuttering power. Without change to dynamic leadership, that power will never be restored to full levels.

—Ramesh Deonaraine

Competition

I have been up against tough competition all my life. I wouldn't know how to get along without it.

—Walt Disney

Thank God for competition. When our competitors upset our plans or outdo our designs, they open infinite possibilities of our own work to us.

—Gil Atkinson

The person who figures out how to harness the collective genius of his or her organization is going to blow the competition away.

—Walter Wriston

The difference of great players is at a certain point in a match they raise their level of play and maintain it. Lesser players play great for a set, but then less.

—Pete Sampras

Training

Because the importance of training is so commonly underestimated, the manager who wants to make a dramatic improvement in organizational effectiveness without challenging the status quo will find a training program a good way to start.

—Theodore Caplow

You can change behavior in an entire organization, provided you treat training as a process rather than an event.

—Edward W. Jones

The question isn't: 'What if we train people and they leave?' The question should be: 'What if we don't train them and they stay?'

—Brian Tracy

Thomas Watson [of IBM] trained, and trained, and trained.

—Peter Drucker

Give a man a fish and he will have a meal. Teach him to catch fish and he will have meals for the rest of his life.

—Lao Tse

No one can attain greatness in any field except through extensive training. The key to this success is self-training—even when you receive training from others, you have to personally orient this training to your specific psychological and learning needs and use it as a basis for training yourself until you attain excellence.

—Ramesh Deonaraine

The best student is the one who understands the importance of self-training and is fully dedicated to it.

—Ramesh Deonaraine

Vision

See the quotes in Chapter 6 under "Vision."

If you want to build a ship, don't drum up people together to collect wood and don't assign them tasks and work, but rather teach them to long for the endless immensity of the sea.

—Saint-Exupery

There is no more powerful engine driving an organization toward excellence and long-range success than an attractive, worthwhile, and achievable vision of the future, widely shared.

—Burt Nanus.

A vision is only an idea or an image of a more desirable future for the organization, but the right vision is an idea so energizing that it in effect jump-starts the future by calling forth the skills, talents and resources to make it happen.

—Burt Nanus.

I believe the real difference between success and failure in a corporation can very often be traced to the question of how

well the organization brings out the great energies and talents of its people. What does it do to help those people find common cause with each other?

—Thomas J. Watson Jr.

6

Mental Power

Mind

Mind is the great lever of all things; human thought is the process by which human ends are ultimately answered.

—Daniel Webster

The mind is its own place, and in itself
Can make a heaven of hell, a hell of heaven.

—Milton

It is not enough to have a good mind; the main thing is to use it well.

—Descartes

The mind is a strange machine which can combine the materials offered it in the most astonishing ways.

—Bertrand Russell

The mind is a dangerous weapon, even to its possessor, if he knows not discreetly how to use it.

—Montaigne

Intuition

Six chief executive officers of major companies interviewed by researchers Harry Levinson and Stuart Rosenthal all expressed the same regret. Walter Wriston of First National City Bank; Thomas J. Watson, Jr., of IBM; Reginal Jones of General Electric; Arthur Sulzberger, Jr., of The New York Times; John Hanley of Monsanto; and Ian K. MacGregor of AMAX each said that he had not followed his intuition as frequently as he could have.

—Charles Garfield

Intuition becomes increasingly valuable in the new information society precisely because there is so much data.

—John Naisbitt

Intuition is a spiritual faculty and does not explain, but simply points the way.

—Florence Scovel Shinn

...we should trust our intuition. I believe that the principles of universal evolution are revealed to us through our intuition...if we combine our intuition and our reason, we can respond in an evolutionary sound way to our problems.

—Jonas Salk

[Intuition] does not denote something contrary to reason, but something outside the province of reason.

—Carl Jung

We know the truth not only by reason but also by the heart.

—Blaise Pascal

Intuition, the highest form of knowing, knowing without being aware of the process of arriving at the conclusion, must

never be confused with the lazy jumping to a conclusion, which is always an unworkable substitute for serious effort.

—Ramesh Deonaraine

I have found that when I listen to my intuition, I am led to places that I would have never gone had I listened only to the logic of my rational mind. And the results have been magical.

—Susan Jeffers

I always remain open to the new information my inner voice may give me about my goal.

—Georgette Mosbacher

Wisdom

The wise don't expect to find life worth living. They make it that way.

—Anonymous

Circumstances are the rulers of the weak; they are but the instruments of the wise.

—Samuel Lover

Wisdom consists not so much in knowing what to do in the ultimate as in knowing what to do next.

—Herbert Hoover

Wisdom is the principal thing; therefore get wisdom; and with all thy getting get understanding.

—Bible

Be happy. It is a way of being wise.

—Colette

Wisdom comes, not from years lived, but from insights gleaned.

—Ramesh Deonaraine

How prone to doubt, how cautious are the wise!

—Homer

Fools rush in where the wise tread carefully.

—English proverb

Wisdom magnifies your mental power, enabling you to separate the relevant from the irrelevant, the real from the unreal.

—Ramesh Deonaraine

Wisdom is the accurate perception of reality.

—Ramesh Deonaraine

Intelligence

A good mind possesses a kingdom.

—Seneca

It is not enough to have a good mind; the main thing is to use it well.

—Descartes

The test of a first-rate intelligence is the ability to hold two opposed ideas in the mind at the same time, and still retain the ability to function.

—F. Scott Fitzgerald

Keen intelligence is like a two-edged sword. It can be used to cut through ignorance or to decapitate the self.

—Sri Yukteswarji

Intelligence is quickness in seeing things as they are.

—George Santayana

Many complain of their looks, but none of their brains.

—Yiddish proverb

Only the unintelligent dog cries for the moon.

—English proverb.

Thought

Our life is what our thoughts make it.

—Marcus Aurelius

My thoughts are my company; I can bring them together, select them, detain them, dismiss them.

—Walter Savage Landor

The highest possible stage in moral culture is when we recognize that we ought to control our thought.

—Charles Darwin

Thinking is hard work. One can't bear burden and ideas at the same time.

—Remy de Gourmont

What is the hardest task in the world? To think.

—Emerson

Many highly intelligent people are poor thinkers. Many people of average intelligence are skilled thinkers. The power of a car is separate from the way the car is driven.

—Edward de Bono

Imagination

...the man who invented the wheel while he was observing another man walking—that is imagination!

—Jacques Lipchitz

Imagination is the highest kite one can fly.

—Lauren Bacall

A rock pile ceases to be a rock pile the moment a single man contemplates it, bearing within him the image of a cathedral.

—Saint-Exupery

Imagination grows by exercise, and contrary to common belief, is more powerful in the mature than in the young.

—Somerset Maugham

Imagination is more important than knowledge.

—Albert Einstein

When you are completely caught up in something, you become oblivious to things around you, or to the passage of time.... [This] frees your unconscious mind and releases your creative imagination.

—Rollo May

Imagination and work are keys that unlock the Kingdom of Heaven and let you bring among your fellows, and be credited for, the bounty you find.

—Ramesh Deonaraine

Imagination without effort is like locating much gold but never digging for it.

—Ramesh Deonaraine

Every great creation begins in the imagination and grows through effort.

—Ramesh Deonaraine

Imagination is the fluidity that keeps the machine of progress roving onward.

—Ramesh Deonaraine

Ideas, Insights

A moment's insight is sometimes worth a life's experience.

—Oliver Wendell Holmes

A single idea, if it is right, saves us the labor of an infinity of experiences.

—Jacques Maritain

Good ideas are not adopted automatically. They must be driven into practice with courageous patience.

—Admiral Hyman Rickover

Great ideas need landing gear as well as wings.

—Adophe Berle, Jr.

Judgment, Decisions

Knowledge is the treasure, but judgment is the treasurer of a wise man.

—William Penn

We are mistaken in believing the mind and the judgment are two separate things; judgment is only the extent of the mind's illumination.

—La Rochefoucald

The roads we take are more important than the goals we announce. Decisions determine destiny.

—Frederick Speakman

Clear thinking without knowledge will not guarantee a sound decision and extensive knowledge without clear thinking is no better.

—A. R. Duncan

The quality of decision is like the well-timed swoop of a falcon which enables it to strike and destroy its victim.

—Sun Tzu

Genius

There is no genius like the genius of energy and activity.

—Donald Mitchell

All the genius I have is the fruit of labor.

—Alexander Hamilton

Genius is one percent inspiration and ninety nine percent perspiration.

—Thomas Edison

If people knew how hard I worked to get my mastery, it wouldn't seem so wonderful after all.

—Michelangelo

A genius? Perhaps, but before I was a genius I was a drudge.

—Paderewski

One of the strongest characteristics of genius is the power of lighting its own fire.

—John W. Forster

God gives you talent. Work transforms talent into genius.

—Anna Pavlova

Genius means little more than the faculty of perceiving in an unhabitual way.

—William James

Genius is the infinite capacity for taking pains.

—Jane Ellice Hopkins

The essence of genius is knowledge of what to overlook.

—William James

Common sense is instinct. Enough of it is genius.

—George Bernard Shaw

Too often we forget that genius...depends upon the data within its reach, that Archimedes could not have devised Edison's inventions.

—Ernest Dimnet

A genius is one who shoots at something no one can see, and hits it.

—Anonymous

To do the best you can each moment is to manifest genius in living.

—Ramesh Deonaraine

Creativity, Inspiration

Just as appetite comes by eating, so work brings inspiration, if inspiration is not discernible at the beginning.

—Igor Stravinsky

When you are completely caught up in something, you become oblivious to things around you, or to the passage of time.... [This] frees your unconscious mind and releases your creative imagination.

—Rollo May

Action always generates inspiration....

—Frank Tibolt

The great composer...does not set to work because he is inspired, but becomes inspired because he is working. Beethoven, Wagner, Bach, and Mozart settled down day after day to the job in hand with as much regularity as an accountant settles down each day to his figures. They didn't waste time waiting for inspiration.

—Ernest Newman

Most of life is routine—dull and grubby. But routine is the momentum that keeps a man going. If you wait for inspiration you'll be standing on the corner after the parade is a mile down the street.

—Ben Nicholas

Man's main task in life is to give birth to himself....

—Erich Fromm

Creative minds have always been known to survive any kind of bad training.

—Anna Freud

Vision

Vision is the art of seeing things invisible.

—Jonathan Swift

Vision needs no special gift or effort, but only the use of a faculty all possess but few employ.

—Colin Wilson

To see clearly is poetry, prophecy, and religion—all in one.

—John Ruskin

The greatest visionary accurately perceives the grand possibilities of how reality can unfold.

—Ramesh Deonaraine

7

Learning

Learning

To learn is a natural pleasure, not confined to philosophers, but common to all men.

—Aristotle

Learning is its own exceeding great reward.

—William Hazlitt

They know enough who know how to learn.

—Henry Adams

The great poem and the deep theorem are new to every reader, and yet are his own experiences, because he himself recreates them.

—Jacob Bronowski

The thirst to know and understand,
A large and liberal discontent;
These are the goods in life's rich hand,
The things that are more excellent.

—Sir William Watson

I am still learning.

—Michelangelo, when he was already
a great artist

The excitement of learning separates youth from old age. As long as you're learning you're not old.

—Rosalyn Yalow

Only those who have learned a lot are in a position to admit how little they know.

—L. Carte

The ultimate aim of learning is wisdom—the accurate perception of reality.

—Ramesh Deonaraine

Frustration in Learning

I think and think for months and years. Ninety-nine times, the conclusion is false. The hundredth time I am right.

—Albert Einstein

I have learned throughout my life as a composer chiefly through my mistakes and pursuit of false assumptions, not by my exposure to founts of wisdom and knowledge.

—Igor Stravinsky

The most important of my discoveries have been suggested to me by my failures.

—Sir Humphry Davy

...I found general relativity very difficult at first and did not make much progress.

—Stephen Hawking,
world-renowned theoretical physicist

I will never forget my first exam [in physics, in graduate school at Columbia University]. It was an open-book exam with five

questions. I couldn't do any of them. By the time I got to number five, I was in a cold sweat.

—Arno Penzias, Nobel Prize
winner in physics.

Knowledge

Knowledge is power.

—Francis Bacon

Without knowledge, life is no more than the shadow of death.

—Moliere

Knowledge, not the eyes, is the true organ of sight.

—Panchatantra

The right to know is like the right to live. It is fundamental and unconditional in its assumption that knowledge, like life, is a desirable thing.

—George Bernard Shaw

Knowledge...is the great sun in the firmament. Life and power are scattered with all its beams.

—Daniel Webster

Knowledge is the only fountain both of the love and the principles of human liberty.

—Daniel Webster

Knowledge...is our best protection against unreasoning prejudice and panic-making fear....

—Franklin D. Roosevelt

Education

The principal goal of education is to create men who are capable of doing new things, not simply of repeating what other generations have done—men who are creative, inventive and discoverers.

—Jean Piaget

Real education consists of drawing the best out of yourself.

—Mahatma Gandhi

The goal of education is the advancement of knowledge and the dissemination of truth.

—John F. Kennedy

Education is the leading of human souls to what is best, and making what is best out of them....

—John Ruskin

Education, properly understood, is that which teaches discernment.

—Joseph Roux

Education...beyond all other devices of human origin, is a great equalizer of the conditions of men....

—Horace Mann

The human mind is our fundamental resource.

—John F. Kennedy

If our education had included training to bear unpleasantness and to let the first shock pass until we could think more calmly, many an unbearable situation would become manageable, and many a nervous illness avoided. There is proverb expressing this. It says, trouble is a tunnel through which we

pass and not a brick wall against which we must break our head.

—Claire Weeks

Formal education will make you a living; self-education will make you a fortune.

—Jim Rohn

Teachers, Professors

I am quite sure that in the hereafter she will take me by the hand and lead me to my proper place.

—Bernard Baruch, on one of
his teachers

One good teacher in a lifetime may sometimes change a delinquent into a solid citizen.

—Philip Wylie

A teacher affects eternity; he can never tell where his influence stops.

—Henry Adams

Teachers, who educate children, deserve more honor than parents, who merely gave them birth; for the latter provided mere life, while the former ensure a good life.

—Aristotle

What nobler employment, or more valuable to the state, than that of the man who instructs the rising generation?

—Cicero

Teachers believe they have a gift for giving; it drives them with the same irrepressible drive that drives others to create a work of art or a market or a building.

—A. Bartlett Giamati

The good teacher…discovers the natural gifts of his pupils and liberates them by the stimulating influence of the inspiration that he can impart. The true leader makes his followers twice the men they were before.

—Stephen Neill

An outstanding teacher can open for you vistas you never knew existed and guide you to a destiny even beyond your dreams.

—Ramesh Deonaraine

School, College, University

There Learning dwells, and Peace is Wisdom's guest.

—Gardner Tucker

The schools of the country are its future in miniature.

—Tehyi Hsieh

The aim of the college, for the individual student, is to eliminate the need in his life for the college; the task is to help him become a self-educating man.

—C. Wright Mills

A university should be a place of light, of liberty, and of learning.

—Disraeli

The task of the university is the creation of the future, so far as rational thought and civilized modes of appreciation can affect the issue.

—Alfred North Whitehead

Men may be born free; they cannot be born wise, and it is the duty of the university to make the free wise.

—Adlai Stevenson

The most important function of education at any level is to develop the personality of the individual and the significance of his life to himself and to others.

—Grayson Kirk

Universities should be safe havens where ruthless examination of realities will not be distorted by the aim to please or inhibited by the risk of displeasure.

—Kingman Brewster

Freedom of inquiry, freedom of discussion, and freedom of teaching—without these a university cannot exist.

—Robert Maynard Hutchins

Exams, Class Rank

Examinations are formidable even to the best prepared, for the greatest fool may ask more than the wisest man can answer.

—Charles Colton

The night before an exam we see with crystal clarity how we could have lived better, prepared more.

—Ramesh Deonaraine

The determination to do better in the future frequently surges as you go through an exam. Keeping this determination is a key to greater achievement.

—Ramesh Deonaraine

I didn't sleep the night before the exam because of nervous tension...so I didn't do very well. I was on the borderline between a first- and a second-class degree, and I had to be interviewed by the examiners to determine which I should get.

—Stephen Hawking, world-renowned
theoretical physicist, on his degree
exam at Oxford.

...after the first year, everyone who came below twentieth in the class was put down to the B stream. This was a tremendous blow to their self-confidence, from which some never recovered. In my first two terms...I came twenty-fourth and twenty-third, but in my third term, I came eighteenth. So I just escaped.

—Stephen Hawking,

The race does not always belong to the swiftest.

—English proverb

Attention

If I have ever made any valuable discoveries, it has been owing more to patient attention than to any other talent.

—Sir Isaac Newton

...the one lesson I have learned is that there is no substitute for paying attention.

—Diane Sawyer

Paying keen attention to anything to which your life should be committed multiplies your power and brings to your consciousness insights, skills, and abilities you never knew were there to be had.

—Ramesh Deonaraine

The whole secret of the study of nature lies in learning how to use one's eyes.

—George Sand

I keep six honest serving-men
They taught me all I know;
Their names are What and Why and When
And How and Where and Who....

—Rudyard Kipling

Preparation, Practice

The will to win is important, but the will to prepare is vital.

—Joe Paterno

In the field of observation, chance favors the prepared mind.

—Louis Pasteur

To be prepared is half the victory.

—Miguel Cervantes

Spectacular achievement is always preceded by spectacular preparation.

—Robert H. Schuller

The general who wins the battle makes many calculations in his temple before the battle is fought. The general who loses makes but few calculations beforehand.

—Sun Tzu

Practice what you know, and it will help to make clear what now you do not know.

—Rembrandt

Fortune favors those who are prepared.

—Anonymous

Luck is a matter of preparation meeting opportunity.

—Oprah Winfrey

Practice makes perfect.

—English proverb

Practice is the true master.

—Latin proverb

If I don't practice one day, I know it; two days, the critics know it; three days, the public knows it.

—Jascha Heifetz, on his music practice

I did practice, every day. I rehearsed every piece I had ever played, note by note, in my mind.

—Liu Chi Kung, explaining his piano
skills after 7 years in prison with no
access to a piano

No one can attain greatness in any field except through extensive training. The key to this success is self-training—even when you receive training from others, you have to personally orient this training to your specific psychological and learning

needs and use it as a basis for training yourself until you attain excellence.

—Ramesh Deonaraine

The best student is the one who understands the importance of self-training and is fully dedicated to it.

—Ramesh Deonaraine

8

Great Pursuits

Art

Art enlarges experience by admitting us to the inner life of others.

—Walter Lippman

Art distills sensation and embodies it with enhanced meaning in memorable form....

—Jacques Barzun

Picture and sculpture are the celebrations and festivities of form.

—Emerson

A picture can become for us a highway between a particular thing and a universal feeling.

—Lawren Harris

Painting is silent poetry, and poetry is painting with the gift of speech.

—Simonides

The object of art is to give life a shape.

—Jean Anouith

Art washes away from the soul the dust of everyday life.

—Picasso

I dream my painting and I paint my dream.

—Vincent van Gogh

Economics

...the ideas of economists...are more powerful than is commonly understood.... Practical [people], who believe themselves to be quite exempt from any intellectual influences, are usually the slaves of some...economist.

—J. M. Keynes

Everybody thinks of economics whether he is aware of it or not. In joining a political party and in casting his ballot, the citizen implicitly takes a stand upon essential economic theories.

—Ludwig von Mises

The complicated analysis which economists...carry through are not mere gymnastic. They are instruments for bettering human life.

—A. C. Pigou

We study economics to learn how not to be deceived by other economists.

—Joan Robinson

[Economics] is a method rather than a doctrine, an apparatus of the mind, a technique of thinking which helps its possessor to draw correct conclusions.

—J. M. Keynes

History

The disadvantage in men not knowing the past is that they do not know the present. History is a hill or high point of vantage, from which alone men see the town in which they live or the age in which they are living.

—G. K. Chesterton

To be ignorant of what occurred before you were born is to remain always a child. For what is the worth of human life, unless it is woven into the life of our ancestors by the records of history?

—Cicero

Man himself is the most important creation and achievement of the continuous human effort, the record of which we call history.

—Erich Fromm

…a page of history is worth a volume of logic.

—Oliver Wendell Holmes

History is a vast early warning system.

—Norman Cousins

We can chart our future clearly and wisely only when we know the path which has led to the present.

—Adlai Stevenson

Wherever men have lived there is a story to be told, and it depends chiefly on the story-teller or historian whether that is interesting or not.

—Henry David Thoreau

History, if thoroughly comprehended, furnishes something of the experience which a man would acquire who should be a contemporary of all ages and a fellow-citizen of all peoples.

—Joseph Roux

Don't brood on what's past, but don't forget it either.

—Thomas Raddall

Those who forget the past are condemned to relive it.

—George Santayana

Literature

Fiction reveals truth that reality obscures.

—Jessamyn West

A novel is never anything but a philosophy put into images.

—Albert Camus

I find biography in every fable I read.

—Emerson

With a pen in my hand I have successfully stormed bulwarks from which others armed with sword and excommunication have been repulsed.

—Georg C. Lichtenberg

I really do inhabit a system in which words are capable of shaking the entire structure of government, where words can prove mightier than ten military divisions.

—Vaclav Havel

Literature is news that stays news.

—Ezra Pound

Literature is the immortality of speech.

—August Wilhelm Von Schlegel

Mathematics

Mathematics, rightly viewed, possesses not only truth, but supreme beauty—a beauty cold and austere, like that of sculpture, without appeal to any part of our weaker nature, without the gorgeous trappings of painting or music, yet sublimely pure, and capable of a stern perfection such as only the greatest art can show.

—Bertrand Russell

The science of pure mathematics, in its modern developments, may claim to be the most original creation of the human spirit.

—Alfred North Whitehead

From the intrinsic evidence of his creation, the Great Architect of the Universe now begins to appear as a pure mathematician.

—Sir James Hopwood Jeans

Music

Music has charms to soothe a savage breast
To soften rocks, or to bend a knotted oak.

—William Congreve

Who hears music, feels his solitude
Peopled at once.

—Robert Browning

Music...can name the unnamable and communicate the unknowable.

—Leonard Bernstein

From Mozart I learnt to say important things in a conversational way.

—George Bernard Shaw

Mozart is sunshine.

—Antonin Dvorak

Music is well said to be the speech of angels.

—Thomas Carlyle

Music is a strange thing. I would almost say it is a miracle. For it stands halfway between thought and phenomenon, between spirit and matter.

—Heinrich Heine

Music produces a kind of pleasure which human nature cannot do without.

—Confucius

Music is the shorthand of emotion.

—Tolstoy

After silence, that which comes nearest to expressing the inexpressible is music.

—Aldous Huxley

Music is another planet.

—Alphonse Daudet

Music is the art of thinking with sounds.

—Jules Combarieu

Where words fail, music speaks.

—Hans Christian Andersen

Philosophy

The object of studying philosophy is to know one's own mind....

—William Ralph Inge

You can't do without philosophy, since everything has its hidden meaning which we must know.

—Maxim Gorky

In philosophy an individual is becoming himself.

—Bernard Lonergan

Philosophy begins in wonder. And at the end, when philosophic thought has done its best, the wonder remains.

—Alfred North Whitehead

To be a philosopher is not merely to have subtle thoughts...but so to love wisdom as to live according to its dictates....

—Thoreau, Henry David

The great philosophers are poets who believe in the reality of their poems.

—Antonio Machado

Let no young man delay the study of philosophy, and let no old man become weary of it; for it is never too early nor too late to care for the well-being of the soul.

—Epicurus

To teach how to live with uncertainty, and yet without being paralyzed by hesitation, is perhaps the chief thing that philosophy in our age can still do for those who study it.

—Bertrand Russell

Poetry

When power narrows the areas of man's concerns, poetry reminds him of the richness and diversity of his experience.

—John F. Kennedy

...poetry is painting with the gift of speech.

—Simonides

The world is never the same once a good poem has been added to it. A good poem helps to change the shape and significance of the universe, helps to extend everyone's knowledge of himself and the world around him.

—Dylan Thomas

The world is so great and rich, and life so full of variety, that you can never lack occasions for great poems.

—Goethe

Poetry is the language in which man explores his own amazement.

—Christopher Fry

Poetry is not an assertion of truth, but the making of that truth more real to us.

—T.S. Eliot

Science, Theory

Science is the most intimate school of resignation and humility, for it teaches us to bow before the seemingly most insignificant of facts.

—Miguel de Unamuno

The truth is, that those who have never entered upon scientific pursuits know not a tithe of the poetry by which they are surrounded.

—Herbert Spencer

Science is the attempt to make the chaotic diversity of our sense-experience correspond to a logically uniform system of thought.

—Albert Einstein

The concern for man and his destiny must always be the chief interest of all technical effort. Never forget this in the midst of your diagrams and equations.

—Albert Einstein

Science is built of facts the way a house is built of bricks; but an accumulation of facts is no more science than a pile of bricks is a house.

—Henri Poincare

There is nothing more practical than good theory.

—Kurt Lewin

Those who are enamored of practice without science are like a pilot who goes into a ship without rudder or compass and never had any certainty where he is going. Practice should always be based upon a sound knowledge of theory.

—Leonardo da Vinci

Books, Reading

Books are the carriers of civilization. Without books, history is silent, literature dumb, science crippled, thought and speculation at a standstill.

—Barbara Tuchman

All that mankind has done, thought, gained or been: it is lying as in magic preservation in the pages of books.

—Thomas Carlyle

Books are humanity in print.

—Barbara Tuchman

Books are the open avenues down which, like kings coming to be crowned, great ideas and inspirations move to the abbey of man's soul. There are some people still left who understand perfectly what Fenelon meant when he said, "If the crowns of all the kingdoms of the empire were laid down at my feet in exchange for my books and my love of reading, I would spurn them all."

—Ernest Dressel North

The real purpose of books is to trap the mind into doing its own thinking.

—Christopher Morley

...if we can read, we can live as many lives and as many kinds of lives as we wish.

—S. I. Hayakawa

A great book should leave you with many experiences.... You live several lives while reading it.

—William Styron

When you sell a man a book you don't sell him just 12 ounces of paper and ink and glue—you sell him a whole new life.

—Christopher Morley

Writing

A writer is somebody for whom writing is more difficult than it is for other people.

—Thomas Mann

Writing is the supreme solace.

—Somerset Maugham

A man may write at any time, if he will set himself doggedly to it.

—Samuel Johnson

No one who cannot limit himself has ever been able to write.

—Nicolas Boileau

Writing has laws of perspective, of light and shade, just as painting does, or music. If you are born knowing them, fine. If not, learn them. Then rearrange the rules to suit yourself.

—Truman Capote

With a pen in my hand I have successfully stormed bulwarks from which others armed with sword and excommunication have been repulsed.

—Georg C. Lichtenberg

I really do inhabit a system in which words are capable of shaking the entire structure of government, where words can prove mightier than ten military divisions.

—Vaclav Havel

9

Adversity

Adversity

If you find a path with no obstacles, it probably doesn't lead anywhere.

—Frank Clark

An obstacle is something you see when you take your eyes off your goal.

—Anonymous

I would not have amounted to anything were it not for adversity. I was forced to come up the hard way.

—J. C. Penney

To appreciate heaven well, t'is good for a man to have some fifteen minutes of hell.

—Will Carleton

It is a rough road that leads to the heights of greatness.

—Seneca

Progress is not created by contented people.

—Frank Tyger

Were it not for slow, painful, and constantly discouraged creative effort, man would be no more than a species of primate living on seeds, fruit, roots, and uncooked flesh.

—James Harvey Robinson

Adversity causes some men to break; others to break records.

—William Ward

Even in the deepest sinking there is the hidden purpose of an ultimate rising. Thus it is for all men, from none is the source of light withheld unless he himself withdraws from it. Therefore the most important thing is not to despair.

—Hasidic saying

Problems are only opportunities in work clothes.

—Henry J. Kaiser

Uncertainty

Uncertainty and mystery are energies of life. Don't let them scare you unduly, for they keep boredom at bay and spark creativity.

—R. I. Fitzhenry

Maturity of mind is the capacity to endure uncertainty.

—John Finley

The central problem of our age is how to act decisively in the absence of certainty.

—Bertrand Russell

Change is not made without inconvenience, even from worse to better.

—Richard Hooker

In Chinese, the word for crisis is **wei ji**, composed of the characters **wei**, which means danger, and **ji**, which means opportunity.

—Jan Wong

There are so many tensions involved in any creative activity…so when there is a catastrophe you never indicate that you think the end of the world has come. You examine it and say, "Well, this is a fine new catastrophe. Now, what else is important today?"

—Goeran Gentele

Circumstances are the rulers of the weak; they are but instruments of the wise.

—Samuel Lover

A diamond is a chunk of coal that made good under pressure.

—Anonymous

As a painter I shall never signify anything of importance. I feel it absolutely.

—Vincent van Gogh

Failure

Defeat can be the first step to something better.

—Edmund Burke

Failure is a part of success. There is no such thing as a bed of roses all your life. But failure will never stand in the way of success if you learn from it.

—Hank Aaron

Good people are good because they have come to wisdom through failure.

—William Saroyan

What is called failure is frequently a necessary foundation for success. Failure, viewed thoughtfully, gives us lessons, ideas, and passion to drive to success.

—Ramesh Deonaraine

I've come to believe that all my past failure and frustration were actually laying the foundation for the understandings that have created the new level of living I now enjoy.

—Anthony Robbins

No life is all success or all failure. The greatest successes failed many times, but they did not give in to despair. They learned from failure, worked hard and intelligently, and went on to great success.

—Ramesh Deonaraine

There is no failure except in no longer trying.

—Elbert Hubbard

There is always another chance.... This thing we call "failure" is not the falling down, but the staying down.

—Mary Pickford

People are failures, not because they are stupid, but because they are not sufficiently impassioned.

—Burt Struthers

Grief

When some great sorrow, like a mighty river,
Flows through your life with peace-
destroying power...
Say to your heart each trying hour:
"This, too, shall pass away."

—Lanta Wilson Smith

The swallows of sorrow may fly overhead, but don't let them nest in your hair.

—Chinese proverb

If you are distressed by anything external, the pain is not due to the thing itself but to your own estimate of it; and this you have the power to revoke at any moment.

—Marcus Aurelius

It is dangerous to abandon oneself to the luxury of grief; it deprives one of courage, and even of the wish for recovery.

—Henri-Frederic Amiel

I must lose myself in action lest I wither in despair.

—Tennyson

Work is the grand cure for all the maladies that ever beset mankind—honest work which you intend getting done.

—Thomas Carlyle

Whatever our grief, many others have likely faced more, over-came, and gone on to live dynamically—supreme examples for us.

—Ramesh Deonaraine

Fear, Nervousness, Anxiety

Throughout my career, nervousness and stage fright have never left me before playing. And each of the thousands of concerts I have played at, I feel as bad as I did the very first time.

—Pablo Casals

One of the great discoveries man makes, one of his great surprises, is to find he can do what he was afraid he couldn't do. Most of the bars we beat against are in ourselves—we put them there and we can take them down.

—Henry Ford

Anxiety is the handmaiden of creativity.

—Chuck Jones

A certain amount of fear is useful, keeping us from engaging in reckless acts, and spurring us to do what is essential for our success.

—Ramesh Deonaraine

A fighter has to know fear.

—Cus D'Amato

Everyone feels fear, nervousness, and anxiety when they have work to do. Those who achieve proceed with their efforts in spite of these fears, and as they make progress, feelings of achievement and success replace fears.

—Ramesh Deonaraine

Those who underachieve through insufficient work let their fear of work prevent them from starting their efforts. The

secret of overcoming fear of work, however, is to start working.

—Ramesh Deonaraine

Most of our obstacles would melt away if, instead of cowering before them, we should make up our minds to walk boldly through them.

—O. S. Marsden

I do not think I am fit for the Presidency.

—Abraham Lincoln

Adaptability, Change

A slender sapling survives a storm by swaying with the wind; a rigid old branch breaks off and dies. We learn much from trees.

—Japanese proverb

Learn to adjust yourself to the conditions you have to endure, but make a point of trying to alter or correct conditions so that they are most favorable to you.

—William Frederick Book

Enjoying success requires the ability to adapt. Only by being open to change will you have a true opportunity to get the most from your talent.

—Nolan Ryan

There are no conditions to which a man cannot become accustomed, especially if he sees that all those around him live in the same way.

—Tolstoy

What is more enthralling to the human mind than this splendid, boundless, colored mutability!—Life in the making?

—David Grayson

When old words die out on the tongue, new melodies break forth from the heart; and where the old tracks are lost, new country is revealed with its wonders.

—Rabindranath Tagore

It is not the strongest of the species that survive, nor the most intelligent, but the one most responsive to change.

—Charles Darwin

10

Home, Family, Relationships

Home, Family

A happy family is but an earlier heaven.

—Sir John Bowring

He is the happiest, be he king or peasant, who finds peace in his home.

—Goethe

Nor need we power or splendor, wide hall or lordly dome; the good, the true, the tender—these form the wealth of home.

—Sarah J. Hale

Home is the place where, when you have to go there,
They have to take you in.

—Robert Frost

Home is not where you live but where they understand you.

—Christian Morgenstern

If I were asked to name the chief benefit of the house, I should say: the house shelters day-dreaming, the house protects the dreamer, the house allows one to dream in peace.

—Gaston Bachelard

He may be President but he still comes home and swipes my socks.

—Joseph Kennedy about his son,
President John F. Kennedy

The presidency is temporary—but the family is permanent.

—Yvonne de Gaulle, wife of French
President Charles de Gaulle

The happiest moments of my life have been the few which I have passed at home in the bosom of my family.

—Thomas Jefferson

Relationships

To be is to be related.

—Cassius J. Keyser

Snowflakes are one of nature's most fragile things, but just look what they can do when they stick together.

—Vesta Kelly

A hundred times every day I remind myself that my inner and outer life depend on the labors of other men, living and dead, and that I must exert myself in order to give in the same measure as I have received.

—Albert Einstein

Some people enter our lives and leave almost instantly. Others stay, and forge such an impression on our heart and soul, we are changed forever.

—Anonymous

What do we live for if it is not to make life less difficult for each other.

—George Eliot

The value of a man should be seen...in what he gives and not in what he is able to receive.

—Albert Einstein

The greatest good you can do for another is not just to share your riches but to reveal him his own.

—Disraeli

The greatest gift we can give one another is rapt attention to one another's existence.

—Sue Atchley Ebaugh

...the only ones among you who will be really happy are those who have sought and found how to serve.

—Albert Schweitzer

Friendship

Friendship makes prosperity more brilliant, and lightens adversity by dividing and sharing it.

—Cicero

Friendship is a strong and habitual inclination in two persons to promote the good and happiness of one another.

—Eustace Budgell

A faithful friend is a strong defense: and he that hath found one hath found a treasure.

—Bible

A friend is a present you give to yourself.

—R. L. Stevenson

A true friend is the greatest of all blessings....

—La Rochefoucauld

You can make more friends in two months by becoming really interested in other people than you can in two years by trying to get other people interested in you.

—Dale Carnegie

There is a magnet in your heart that will attract true friends. That magnet is unselfishness, thinking of others first....

—Paramahansa Yogananda

Trouble is a sieve through which we sift our acquaintances. Those too big to pass through are our friends.

—Arlene Francis

Great friendship is never without anxiety.

—Marquise de Sevigne

The friendship that can come to an end never really began.

—Publilius Syrus

Friendship is almost always the union of a part of one mind with a part of another; people are friends in spots.

—George Santayana

Love

The ultimate lesson all of us have to learn is **unconditional love**, which includes not only others but ourselves as well.

—Elisabeth Kubler-Ross

Of all earthly music, that which reaches furthest into heaven is the beating of a truly loving heart.

—Henry Ward Beecher

There is nothing so loyal as love.

—Alice Cary

Love is a fruit in season at all times and within reach of every hand.

—Mother Teresa

Love is friendship set to music.

—Pollock

A loving heart is the truest wisdom.

—Charles Dickens

We may give without loving but we cannot love without giving.

—Anonymous

Love is the only sane and satisfactory answer to the problems of human existence.

—Erich Fromm

11

Conclusion

If you have read the preceding chapters, congratulations! You have taken an important step toward acquiring the six primary qualities that ensure dynamic living and being inspired to manifest them in key areas of your life. Strive to always be aware that:

> The privilege of a lifetime is being who you are.
>
> —Joseph Campbell

> For if there is a sin against life, it consists perhaps not so much in despairing of life as in hoping for another life and in eluding the implacable grandeur of this life.
>
> —Albert Camus

> To be what we are, and to become what we are capable of becoming, is the only end of life.
>
> —R. L. Stevenson

These quotes are from the first section of Chapter 1. They depict the first of the six primary qualities that are the foundation of all worthy achievement. In the Introduction you were told that as you manifest these qualities in your life, you would:

- Become more focused and purposeful
- See more clearly the unique contributions you can make in your daily life

- Begin to find ways of getting better opportunities and of coping more intelligently with adversity
- Sense more power within you to give you the drive and determination to set and achieve worthy goals
- Become more action-oriented, energetic and enthusiastic
- Have a more wholesome view of life and of your role in it
- Have more rewarding human relationships

I believe that as you put into practice the principles and attitudes inspired by the powerful quotes in this book, you will attain these benefits. You will become energized and dynamic, your life will become more beautiful, and in those wonderful words of John Keats:

A thing of beauty is a joy for ever:
Its loveliness increases....

About the Author

Dr. Ramesh Deonaraine has a reputation for giving very inspirational speeches, lectures and guidance and has received many rave reviews for his presentations before a variety of audiences.

He received the Emily Gregory Award for Excellence in Teaching at Barnard College, Columbia University. In twenty-seven years, he was the only Economics Professor to have received this annual award. He holds several academic degrees, including a Ph.D. in Economics and a Master of International Affairs from Columbia University, and he was a diplomat at the United Nations and in Moscow.

He is currently President of Global Management Solutions, Inc., which has received high praise for consulting services it has provided to well-known corporations. He lives in New York City.

Index

0-595-28855-3

Made in the USA
Lexington, KY
17 February 2012